The LIVERPOOL Cook Book

Including Wirral and Merseyside.
A celebration of the amazing food & drink on our doorstep.
Featuring over 50 stunning recipes.

The Liverpool Cook Book

©2016 Meze Publishing. All rights reserved.

First edition printed in 2016 in the UK.

ISBN: 978-1-910863-15-2

Thank you to: Marc Wilkinson, Paul Askew

Compiled by: Lisa Pullen

Written by: Karen Dent, Kerre Chen, Phil Turner

Photography by:
Tim Green (www.timgreenphotographer.co.uk)

Edited by: Rachel Heward, Phil Turner

Designed by: Matt Crowder, Marc Barker,
Paul Cocker

PR: Kerre Chen

Cover art: Luke Prest, www.lukeprest.com

Contributors: Sarah Koriba, Bethan Littley

Printed by Bell & Bain Ltd, Glasgow

Published by Meze Publishing Limited
Unit S8 & S9 Global Works
Penistone Road
Sheffield S6 3AE
Web: www.mezepublishing.co.uk
Tel: 0114 275 7709
Email: info@mezepublishing.co.uk

FOREWORD

It is a great privilege to be given the opportunity to introduce the purveyors and cooks who are making a difference to our own regional culinary landscape in Merseyside, and it's wonderful to see the publisher capturing their passion in the following pages for you to discover and enjoy.

The fast-beating heart of Merseyside is Liverpool, a city bold in its cultural scene with such incredible offerings in the arts, music, theatres and art galleries, not to mention the stunning architecture that's to be found in and around the city and beyond.

A more recent art form to add to our attractions is the cosmopolitan cuisine now available in the region, from well-crafted dim sum, to Indian street food, or a plate of authentic tapas. We are people proud of our diversity, heritage and warmth. Produce too is passion driven and quality is gaining momentum, with producers making this county an exciting and vibrant place to live – and luckily for me, one to take great advantage of.

One can witness in these pages the culinary voices that make Merseyside a tourist destination of choice and a melting pot of creativity and individuality. Food and drink continues to evolve and a great reflection of this is the Liverpool food and drink festival in Sefton Park, attracting over 45,000 visitors each year.

I must also convey to you, the reader, the unique warmth, generosity, hospitality and general good humour that greets visitors from near and far. The genuinely positive spirited community in Merseyside is very dear to my own heart and you cannot fail to feel the optimism and pride people have in this great city.

It is a city of creativity and culture with a deep, respected history. We are evolving at a great rate of knots; not only in the city centre but Merseyside as a whole is going from strength to strength, thanks to the type of people you will read about as you turn the pages of this book.

I hope you enjoy the insights into our fantastic culinary city and region, and as one of the passionate individuals pushing forward to create amazing tastes for you to enjoy, I very much look forward to welcoming you to Merseyside.

Marc Wilkinson

Chef patron, Fraiche

FOREWORD

Liverpool is a city undergoing a culinary transformation. Our famous port city,
with its rich and diverse cultural heritage, deserves a food and restaurant scene
that it can genuinely be proud of. We are, after all, a city of passion and fun, a city
of firsts and a city that knows how to enjoy itself and deliver
legendary hospitality.

I'm delighted that many of the recipes that have helped to shape the city's culinary renaissance are now recorded in this book for you to recreate at home. From the simple and straightforward to some of the more complex dishes that grace our restaurant tables. It is my hope that making them in the comfort of your own home will ignite a passion for the culinary arts as it did for me many years ago.

I have been fortunate that my love for food has enabled me to travel and experience food and culture across the globe. My passion was first ignited in my early years accompanying my father, a sea captain, to the spice markets of Dubai and then the fish and produce markets of Singapore before working in New York as a sous chef.

I remember those experiences as if they were yesterday, the vibrancy of colour, taste and smell. Those early experiences developed my passion for food and set the foundations for a successful career that enabled me to realise my dream of opening a fine dining restaurant in the city I call home. I realised that dream in 2014 when I opened The Art School Restaurant.

My focus as chef patron today is, as it always has been, using the very best quality fresh local ingredients sourced responsibly and used at their seasonal best. Our city and surrounding region is blessed with some of the finest local food producers. Growing, producing, rearing and harvesting the best asparagus, samphire, herbs, honey, cheese, game, fish and meat.

Their knowledge and dedication ensures we have a plentiful local larder of seasonal fare, while your continued support of them helps them to thrive and grow and helps to ensure our food culture continues to develop.

Enjoy this book, give all of the recipes a try and don't be afraid to create your own. Who knows, you may just end up in the next edition!

Paul Askew

Chef patron, The Art School

Take a gastronomic tour of
LIVERPOOL

Flavours from around the world and ingredients from close to home combine to create an incredible fusion of foods in one city.

As one of the great English sea ports that once brought in people, goods and wealth from around the world, it's little wonder that Liverpool today is such a multicultural city. This diversity is reflected in its cuisine and in the sheer choice a diner is faced with. It's quite possible to eat your way around the world without setting foot outside the city.

Even Liverpool's adopted dish Scouse has its roots overseas. Scouse comes from 'lobscouse', a beef or lamb stew that originated in Northern Europe and found its way to Liverpool with sailors coming into the busy port.

As the gateway to the Atlantic, Liverpool became home to a large number of Irish and Welsh settlers. The city also boasts Britain's oldest black community, dating to the early 1700s, and Europe's oldest Chinese community which has existed since the 19th century. Today, there are also significant Asian, Latin American and Malaysian communities in the city too.

Little wonder then that contemporary Liverpool has a real multicultural buzz which is reflected in the amazing choice of food you'll find here. In The Liverpool Cookbook, we're showcasing some of the very best, from Brazilian and Peruvian restaurants, to Italian street food and authentic French bread and pastries, through to modern British classics, honest to goodness great cakes and afternoon teas with a twist.

The quality of ingredients available – superb livestock from neighbouring Wales and Lancashire, locally caught fish and shellfish and locally grown vegetables – have also played a part in putting Liverpool on the foodie map. Within these pages you'll find inspiration for new dishes from some of the very best delis, butchers and fishmongers you'll come across anywhere, and discover fresh ways of using local ingredients and the very best of liquid refreshments are in here too, from craft ales to locally-produced gin.

As well as the international flavours, you'll find in the book, there are also plenty of homegrown recipes too. If you're after the perfect Scouse recipe, we have the ultimate from the pub that's known as 'the home of Scouse'. If you're after a great cake to treat the family to for tea, a hearty weekend brunch or a show-stopper for a three-course dinner party, you'll find the recipes you need – all with a special Liverpool flavour.

Dive into the pages of The Liverpool Cookbook to start a new gastronomic journey and discover new venues in and around this fantastic city.

Cheers!

CONTENTS

Soul of CUBA

Alma de Cuba, an island in the heart of the city, an independent spirit that leaves a lasting impression.

Alma de Cuba was formerly St. Peters Catholic Church back in 1788. It was the oldest surviving Catholic Church in Liverpool until its closure in 1978. After a period of disuse, the building was taken over by Urban Splash and is now the internationally acclaimed restaurant and bar, Alma de Cuba. It has been through a fair few renovations in its time but the fact that it was previously a church is still visible, the conversion has been tastefully done and the six stained glass windows that were added in 1903 still remain to this day.

Every weekend and bank holiday they are packed to the rafters with both locals and tourists to witness the famous petal shower. At the strike of 11pm, a samba song comes on which is the signal for a blizzard of petals to float down from the restaurant balconies onto the bar floor below. This is also the cue for the samba dancers to come out and strut their stuff across tables in extravagant outfits. Alma de Cuba means 'soul of Cuba' and this is depicted well with the carnival atmosphere and stunning surroundings, creating an amazing ambience that customers are in awe of whether it is their first or hundredth visit.

But that's not the only thing worth shouting about; Alma de Cuba combines an eclectic and broad range of cuisines with South American and Caribbean influences in their food, one of the favourites being the pan roasted Johnson & Swarsbrick duck breast dish which you can make yourself with the recipe overleaf. Head chef Luke Creedon uses local produce where he can and changes the specials board weekly to keep the diners on their toes.

"Each member of the team is talented and passionate about what they do and we always aim to go the extra mile," he says.

Another speciality of theirs is the Sunday Service Gospel Brunch, where a variety of homemade Sunday dishes are served including roast dinners, fish & chips, Cuban breakfasts and eggs Benedict. This is accompanied by the impassioned sounds of their live gospel choir, Soulful Voices, singing all the classics.

Good location, good atmosphere and good food – Alma de Cuba has it all.

Alma De Cuba

PAN SEARED JOHNSON & SWARSBRICK DUCK BREAST WITH SWEET POTATO ROSTI & RED WINE JUS

Head chef Luke Creedon and his kitchen team work hard to ensure all of the ingredients they use are locally-sourced, freshly-prepared and homemade. Chef's tip: when cooking the duck breast, place skin-side down in a cold pan with no oil and on a low heat. – this always gives the best results!

Preparation time: 45 minutes | Cooking time: 7 hours | Serves 4

Ingredients

4 large duck breasts

Pak choi, 1 head per person

For the red wine jus:

2 carrots

2 onions

Celery, 1 head

Rosemary, 1 sprig

Thyme, 1 sprig

Garlic, 1 clove

500g chicken bones

2 bottles of red wine, preferably merlot

For the sweet potato rosti:

150g butter

Rosemary, 1 sprig

Thyme, 1 sprig

Garlic, 1 clove

4 large sweet potatoes, peeled

3 large white potatoes, any brand will do

Salt and pepper

½ tsp five-spice

For the rhubarb and ginger chutney:

50g butter

500g forced rhubarb

50g soft brown sugar

50g stem ginger

Method

For the red wine jus

Roughly dice and sweat the vegetables in large saucepan with the rosemary, thyme and garlic. Add the chicken bones, top with water and simmer for 5-6 hours, making sure to regularly skim the fat from the surface. Once infused, lift the veg and bones from the stock then pass it through a sieve and scoop away any remaining fat. Add two bottles of red wine and reduce by three quarters, continuing to skim. Once reduced, remove the pan from the heat and allow to chill.

For the duck:

To your own taste, lightly season the duck breasts with salt and pepper. Set skin-side down, without oil, into a cold pan and place over a low heat. Once golden brown, place in the oven at 190°c degrees for 7-8 minutes. When cooked, remove from the oven and leave to rest for 2-3 minutes before serving.

Next half the pak choi and rinse. Boil in salted water for 2-3 minutes.

For the sweet potato rosti

Melt the butter in a pan with the rosemary, thyme and garlic. Next grate the four sweet potatoes and three large white potatoes. Add to this the butter mix along with some salt, pepper and half a teaspoon of five-spice. Once infused, wrap the mix in a tea towel and squeeze to drain. Gently flatten the drained mix into a patty shape, and cook in a frying pan with a dash of oil for one minute on each side. Season and place in the oven at 180°c degrees for 4-5 minutes.

For the rhubarb and ginger chutney

Melt 50g of butter in a saucepan. Chop the rhubarb into ½ cm pieces and add to the butter along with the sugar and ginger. Cook over a low heat for 10-15 minutes. Taste and add more sugar if required.

To serve to restaurant standard, view the adjacent image. Enjoy!

A little piece of france in
LIVERPOOL

Visit bakery and patisserie Artisane or order wholesale from sister company The French Corner for a taste of authentic French baking at its very best.

Artisane brings a real flavour of France to Liverpool – and an indulgent one at that. Having opened in March 2016, Artisane is packed with sweet and savoury pastries – pain au chocolat, croissants, cheese twists – plus a massive patisserie selection including bespoke large occasion cakes. Traditional French bread, sandwiches, savoury takeaway dishes, and the special Artisane baguette named in honour of the shop, will also tempt the taste buds.

Anne-Louise Bouffard-Roupe and business partner Alexa Bourgois fulfilled a long-term ambition when Artisane first opened its doors. Having seen how their other halves worked, they were the ones who suggested opening a shop.

Artisane is the brainchild of sister company, The French Corner, which supplies wholesale to many of the city's restaurants and bars across the North West.

The French bakers in charge of supplying Artisane are Anne-Louise's husband Walter Bouffard-Roupe and Alexa's other half, Hakim Benyoub, and their team at The French Corner – the French bakery and wholesaler they set up more than a decade ago.

Walter and Hakim, both French – "worked every single night for a long, long time". Today, there is a team of 15 bakers and the business supplies a huge range of customers with its authentic French breads, brioche buns and patisserie products. They include restaurants, hotels, bars, cafés and some big name clients including the Echo Arena, Bolton Wanderers Football Club and the bread for Liverpool FC players' training ground. But it is the customers that The French Corner has had from the beginning that the team is thankful to.

"Without them, we wouldn't be where we are today," explains Anne-Louise.

"We knew that we wanted to open a shop and Artisane itself was three years in the making.

"We did a number of market research exercises, the main one being farmers markets. We have had a presence for the last 10 years up and down the country, it has been hard work but it helped to define Artisane and the products that we have on sale. We were able to speak directly to our target audience on a number of levels."

From here, Artisane was born and it took a number of years to get it off the ground, discover the brand and make it happen.

Anne-Louise said: "Everyone who comes in says it's like a piece of France in the heart of south Liverpool, which is exactly what we all wanted."

Artisane and The French Corner
PAIN AU CHOCOLAT

Made the authentic French way, you can also use this dough to make croissants.

Preparation time: 3-4 hours | Cooking time: 15 minutes | Makes 24

Ingredients

1kg plain flour

20g salt

50g yeast

100g sugar

500ml water

1 egg

30g butter

Valrhona chocolate stick

500g butter, for the folding

Method

For the dough

Mix all of the ingredients together (except for the butter and chocolate for the folding) in a food mixer on the lowest speed for 4 minutes until the dough is firm.

Then knead (on the second speed of your mixer) the dough for 8-10 minutes, only stopping to mix it when the dough temperature is between 24-25˚c.

Flatten the dough onto a baking tray and freeze for 30 minutes (make sure that you turn the dough over after 15 minutes).

Fold the dough with the butter, ensuring that the dough is extremely cold.

Rest for 30 minutes in the fridge. Then give it a single fold.

Rest in the fridge for 30 minutes.

For the pain au chocolat

Roll out the dough to a 5mm thickness.

Cut the dough into a rectangular shape, approximately 8.5cm by 14cm.

Shape with 2 chocolate sticks inside for each pain au chocolat. Valrhona chocolate sticks are the very best and this is what we use at Artisane.

Place on a baking tray and brush with egg wash.

You then need to prove your pain au chocolat creations for a period of 2-2.5 hours at 22˚c.

Brush with egg wash again and bake in a preheateded oven at 180˚c for 15 minutes.

Destination DINING

Fine dining in a relaxed atmosphere with quality local food cooked by one of Liverpool's top chefs is The Art School's signature style.

Once the home for destitute children in 1888, then the life drawing and sculpture studio for Liverpool John Moores University, The Art School is fast gaining a reputation as Liverpool's premier fine dining restaurant since opening in 2014.

Headed by chef patron Paul Askew, a North West food champion and fellow of the Royal Academy of Culinary Arts, the restaurant majors in local and seasonal food.

Paul, a pioneer of the Liverpool restaurant scene, is passionate about the provenance of his ingredients and works with a number of local suppliers and growers to secure the very best quality produce for the restaurant's menus.

Delightfully visual with a well-balanced complexity of flavours, each of the dishes is refined and rigorously tested before it's added to the menu.

Paul's passion for the culinary arts extends beyond running The Art School restaurant and he can often be found in the local catering colleges supporting the development of the next generation of chefs through master classes and apprenticeship opportunities.

In just two years, The Art School has frequently topped Liverpool's TripAdvisor and Open Table restaurant ratings, and has been recognised by the Good Food Guide and by the Michelin Guide as the city's best restaurant.

Diners can choose from the prix fixe, excellence and tasting menus, plus vegetarian, vegan and pescatarian versions – a unique offering in fine dining circles.

The restaurant is popular with groups and couples for celebrations, as well as business people lunching in the city centre. It's also making a name for itself as a destination restaurant for diners arriving at Liverpool's cruise liner terminal and visiting the city for business, sport or pleasure.

The restaurant prides itself in the attention to the small details in food and service. The team describe this as "The Art School way", so as well as perfectly balanced plates of food, guests are provided with a choice of sunglasses on sunny days and there's even a selection of reading glasses should you forget yours.

The Art School

LOIN AND CONFIT OF LAKE DISTRICT RABBIT

Served with baby leaf spinach, girolles, Shortwood Hall Farm vegetables and tarragon jus, this is a starter that's sure to impress your dinner party guests.

Preparation time: 45 minutes | Cooking time: 4 hours, including making the stock | Serves 4

Ingredients

1 whole rabbit, skinned

250g spinach, washed

8-10 girolles mushrooms

2 baby carrots

Seasonal baby vegetables, such as turnip, leek or fennel

½ litre duck fat

Maldon sea salt

Sprig of thyme

2 garlic cloves

½ lemon

For the stock:

1 large onion

1 large carrot

1 fennel bulb

Bouquet garni, parsley, tarragon

2 litre water

Fennel seeds

For the tarragon jus:

Reduced rabbit stock

Fresh tarragon to taste

500ml double cream

50g butter

Maldon sea salt to taste

Method

For the rabbit

Place the seasoned trimmed loin of rabbit in a hot thick bottomed sauté pan with a splash of vegetable oil. Brown on all sides for 1-2 minutes then add butter to foam for a further minute. Allow to rest for 2 minutes before carving on to the dish.

Remove the legs of the rabbit and salt for 30 minutes in Maldon sea salt, thyme, garlic and lemon, rinse, then confit in duck fat ensuring the legs are completely covered. Cook for 2½ hours at 150°c.

Once cooked, set aside to rest and cool for 15-20 minutes. Strip the meat off the bones, shred and set aside for service.

Sauté the spinach and the rest of the vegetables and add the shredded confit leg. Combine and set aside ready for plating.

For the rabbit stock

Remove the fillet and any sinew from the rabbit and place in a stock pot with the bouquet garni. Bring to the boil, remove any of the frothy residue from the surface and simmer for 2 hours.

For the tarragon jus

Pass the liquid from the stock pot through a sieve, reduce the sauce by half then add 500ml cream and 50g of butter. Bring to the boil and gently reduce to create a natural sauce of the right consistency. Add tarragon to taste, pass through a sieve and keep warm ready for service. This is the essence of the rabbit.

The Art School

FILLET OF PETERHEAD HAKE

Served with lemon, capers, Southport potted shrimp and parsley butter, with Pommes Mousseline, buttered Dee Estuary samphire, carrot and leek.

Preparation time: 10 minutes | Cooking time: 35 minutes | Serves 4

Ingredients

4 hake fillets, approx. 150–200g each

200g Dee Estuary samphire

Baby carrots, julienned

Baby leeks, julienned

For the pommes mousseline:

4–5 large potatoes – Cyprus /Jersey are ideal

Double cream

Salt and pepper

25g butter

For the sauce

2 pots of potted shrimp

1 beef tomato, diced and deskinned

1 shallot, finely diced

50g capers

Fresh mint, finely chopped

Fresh parsley, finely chopped

Butter with lemon zest

Espelette seasoning

Method

For the pommes mousseline

Cut the potatoes into portions, cover with water and bring to the boil. Simmer for 15 minutes until cooked through. Strain and place them back in to the pan to remove the moisture. Gradually add some cream and butter and mix with a hand blender until smooth. Season to taste and keep warm ready for plating.

For the sauce

Add the diced shallot and tomato to the pan, then add the remaining herbs, butter and lemon zest and gently heat.

Add the potted shrimp, capers and Espelette seasoning. Keep warm ready for plating.

For the hake

Preheat the pan until smoke-point, season the hake skin side and place skin side down on the pan with vegetable oil for 1 minute to 1 minute 30 seconds. Place under the grill for 3-4 minutes on a medium to high heat. Remove and keep warm.

Allow the pan to cool slightly so as not to brown the liquid, add a knob of butter and cover the fish. Serve immediately.

For the samphire and julienne vegetables

Baste the samphire and julienne vegetables with butter and oil and sweat for 3-4 minutes on a medium heat.

The Art School

SEVILLE ORANGE AND OCUMARE DARK CHOCOLATE TRUFFLE TORTE

Served with a roasted hazelnut meringue, mango gel, fresh marinated mango and lime zest, this is a flavour-packed pudding that is worth the preparation.

Preparation time: 25 minutes | Cooking time: time 4-5 hours or preferably overnight | Serves 4

Ingredients

For the torte sponge:

30g sugar

1 egg

22.5g plain flour

7.5g cocoa powder

For the torte mousse:

137.5g 70% dark Ocumare chocolate

250ml cold double cream

37.5ml water

1 orange zest

1½ gelatine leaf

18.5g sugar

For the mango purée:

125g mango purée (from fresh mango pulp)

1.25g agar agar (vegetarian thickening agent)

For the hazelnut meringues:

25g egg whites (1 egg)

50g caster sugar

25g roasted ground hazelnuts

For the mango jelly:

125g mango purée

1½ gelatine leaf

Method

For the torte sponge

Whisk the sugar and eggs in the mixer with the ribbon whisk attachment. When it's at ribbon stage, remove the bowl, sift in the flour and cocoa powder and fold in carefully with your hands to keep the air in.

Spread the mix into a flat loaf tin and bake at 160°c for approximately 7 minutes. The sponge should bounce back when you lightly touch it.

Remove the sponge and cool on a wire rack. When cooled, line the tray with cling film and return the sponge to the base.

For the torte mousse

Place the gelatine in cold water to soften. Add the water, orange zest and sugar to a pan and set aside.

Add the cream to the mixing bowl and whisk until it's the consistency of a thick pouring cream. Set aside. Melt the chocolate in a bowl over simmering water.

Bring the water, orange zest and sugar mixture to the boil, add the softened gelatine and make sure it's all dissolved. Carefully pour the warm water, orange zest and sugar mix into the chocolate and, using a spatula, mix together to create a ganache. Don't over mix or the mixture will split.

The chocolate mix should be around 40°c. Add one third of the cream and carefully fold in and then carefully fold in the rest, ensuring the mix doesn't split. This is a crucial stage of the dish so take great care in preparation.

For the mango purée

Bring the purée to the boil, add the agar and whisk. Bring mix to the boil again and then pour into a lined tray with cling film. Place in the fridge to set. Remove the mixture and blend together until smooth.

For the hazelnut meringues

Whisk egg whites till light and fluffy, adding the sugar gradually. Once at a meringue stage, pipe neatly onto a tray and sprinkle the roasted hazelnut crumb on top.

Place in the oven at 100°c for 20 minutes.

For the mango jelly

Put gelatine in cold water to soften. Bring the mango purée to a simmer (don't boil), add the gelatine leaves and mix well. Pass through a sieve and place in a container lined with cling film to set in the fridge. Once set, remove and cut into even cubes, ready to garnish as per photo.

The Wirral's
HIDDEN GEM

Tucked away in an old lock-up, down a side street in West Kirby, Aubergine is certainly worth seeking out when you're on the Wirral.

Aubergine's owners Andrew and May Mahon have been at the helm since 2011 and were customers at the café before they took it on. Today, Aubergine – named after the restaurant that launched Gordon Ramsay's career – is a café with a twist, where you'll find much more than the usual tea, sandwiches and cakes.

May said: "Aubergine has become a place for foodies in the know. Customers frequently refer to us as a 'hidden gem', a place where you can enjoy a hearty cooked breakfast or a healthy lunch. Or, if you're looking for something a little bit special, we offer afternoon tea but with a modern twist.

"Our staff are a fantastically talented and committed team. We're fortunate to employ some of the most skilful local young chefs who have creative freedom to produce some really delicious dishes. Members of our kitchen team have worked in Michelin-starred kitchens and multiple rosette establishments across the country and our head chef, Ben Costello, was Cheshire Young Chef of the Year 2014."

Fresh local and seasonal ingredients are at the heart of the Aubergine philosophy with meat and fish sourced from specialist suppliers such as Neve Fleetwood, hand-crafted breads from Born & Bread, Anglesey sea salt from Halen Môn and free-range Appleby Eggs delivered to the café every few days fresh from the farm. As a licensed premises you'll also find local gins on the drinks menu, including Wirral Gin.

Hearty breakfasts, lunches and afternoon teas are all cooked from scratch on the premises. Aubergine's menu is seasonal and changes frequently to showcase the best available local ingredients. There is a great choice of vegetarian, vegan and gluten-free options available too.

The café is justly famous for its indulgent afternoon tea, with one customer describing it as 'better than The Ritz', and the café's cakes are lovingly baked by supplier Yasmin, who featured on the Great British Bake Off.

May said: "Yasmin would've gone all the way if it wasn't for some pesky macarons!

"We continually aim to offer traditional, affordable, classic dishes. Being based in a seaside town it's only right that we offer one of our nation's favourite fish dishes: gin battered fish and thrice cooked chips. For vegetarians we offer gin battered halloumi."

Customers come to Aubergine for a warm welcome, good service and wholesome food, all served up in a cosy neighbourhood café. Be prepared to queue, with just 10 tables inside and a few outside the café can get busy, but it's worth the wait.

Andrew said: "My wife and I have created the sort of place where our friends and family like to spend time; a space where good quality, fresh food is at its heart."

"No act of kindness, no matter how small, is ever wasted"
- aesop

Come In
WE'RE
OPEN

Aubergine Café

AUBERGINE CAFE
WEST KIRBY

Aubergine Café

GIN BATTERED FISH AND THRICE COOKED CHIPS

Crunchy thrice cooked chips served with a gin and tonic infused batter makes a
tasty alternative to this traditional favourite.

Preparation time: 30 minutes | Cooking time: 30-40 minutes | Serves 2-3

Ingredients

For the batter

3 egg whites

35ml Wirral Gin

300ml tonic water

1 tsp baking powder

½ tsp cornflour

250g self-raising flour

For the pea purée

300g frozen petit pois

1 white onion

1 garlic clove

1 bunch of fresh mint

500ml vegetable stock

For the tartar sauce

200g good quality mayonnaise

3 medium gherkins

1 tbsp capers

1 lemon

Chives

Parsley

1 egg hard-boiled

Method

For the thrice cooked chips

Wash and peel the potatoes and slice into 1.5 cm chips. Rinse thoroughly under cold water for 3-4 minutes.

Place into a large pan and cover with water. Bring to the boil and simmer for 5-6 minutes. Drain well and rinse until cold.

Carefully arrange onto a lined tray and refrigerate until chilled.

Preheat the fryer to 140°c. Blanch the chips for 20 minutes – the oil will stop bubbling when they are ready.

For the pea purée

Thinly slice and sauté the onion, then add the garlic, stock and peas. Bring to the boil and simmer for 2-3 minutes. Add the mint.

Strain the peas. Blend, adding the cooking liquid gradually, to achieve the right consistency. Season with salt and pepper. Place back onto the tray and refrigerate again until chilled.

For the tartar sauce

Finely dice the gherkins, capers, egg and soft herbs. Combine all ingredients to make the tartar sauce with lemon zest to taste.

For the fish

Turn the fryer to 190°c. Make the batter by whisking the egg whites until light and fluffy. Add the gin and tonic followed by the dry ingredients and continue to whisk.

Coat the fish in the batter and fry for 3-4 minutes until golden. Turn over and cook for a further 3-4 minutes. Keep warm.

Fry the chips for 3-4 minutes until golden, remove and season immediately with Halen Môn Charcoal Sea Salt.

To serve

Serve the fish and chips alongside the tartar sauce and pea purée with a wedge of fresh lemon.

Aubergine Café
EGGY BREAD

Our eggy bread has become one of our best sellers yet is so simple to make. You could also try topping it with crisp bacon and maple syrup or grilled peaches and vanilla yoghurt…many options, all delicious!

Preparation time: 10 minutes | Cooking time: 50 minutes | Serves 4

Ingredients

Brioche loaf

75g natural yoghurt

50g butter

Icing sugar, for dusting

For the batter

4 whole eggs

4 egg yolks

250ml milk

100ml double cream

½ tsp vanilla extract

50g caster sugar

For the berry compote

250g mixed frozen berries

2 tsp vanilla syrup

2 tsp water

100g caster sugar

For the cinnamon sugar

100g sugar

2 tsp cinnamon

Method

First make the berry compote. Add all the ingredients to a shallow pan, bring to the boil and simmer for 45 minutes or until thickened. Remove from the heat and chill immediately.

Combine the sugar and cinnamon together.

To make the batter whisk the egg yolks and sugar together until smooth. Combine with the whole eggs and remaining ingredients.

Slice the brioche into 1.5cm pieces.

Transfer the batter to a shallow tray and add the brioche. Soak for 1 minute then turn over and soak for a further 30 seconds.

Meanwhile, place a non-stick frying pan onto a low-medium heat. Place a small amount of oil in the pan and fry the brioche for 3 minutes. Flip over and fry for a further 1-2 minutes until golden.

Add the cold butter to the pan and when it begins to brown nappe over the French toast.

Remove from the heat and dust immediately with cinnamon sugar.

To serve

Top 2 pieces of French toast with a generous helping of natural yoghurt and berry compote. Dust with icing sugar.

A little piece of
LEBANON

Sitting in the hustle and bustle of Bold Street – this lovingly crafted restaurant is from start to finish an experience of the Mediterranean.

It all started out at the Liverpool Christmas markets where business partners Amine and Otto decided to serve Lebanese street food to the masses. Their innovative yet traditional food was a huge hit which gave them the drive and inspiration to open their first Lebanese restaurant in 2013. The name Bakchich meaning 'loose change' came from their principal message behind their ethos – value for money.

The space is filled with bright, funky colours from the vibrant ingredients and spices on display to the tiles which originally came from the mosaic floor of their grandparent's house in Marrakesh. For Amine, it is not just the food that is important, he wanted to create an environment that would bring people of all backgrounds and beliefs together, to unite communities and educate them on the Arabic food culture, hospitality and traditions.

"Our food is fashionable in all capitals of the world but I would like to revolutionise the Lebanese cuisine throughout the North West, I want to see it as popular as the Italian food in the UK," says Otto. Their mixed grills, falafels, mezze platters and shawarmas are just a few of the many dishes that

are loved at Bakchich. They have an amazing breakfast and dessert menu and they also cater for vegetarians and vegans. "It's great that people are getting more adventurous with food now, Lebanese food is all about sharing and I love that it brings people together," says Mehdi Outaaraft, Bakchich's managing director.

Bakchich pride themselves on how fresh and healthy everything is, all the food is prepared right in front of you in an open kitchen so what you see (and smell) is what you get. Every chef they recruit is sent to the Tabbakh academy to learn their style of cooking so you are definitely in good hands. But if that wasn't reassuring enough, renowned Moroccan chef Mohammed Daifi who has worked at numerous prestigious establishments and has prepared meals for royalty and celebrities is also the executive chef behind the gastronomic team at the restaurant.

The success of Bakchich has lead to the opening of a second site in Manchester and the team hope to continue delivering a unique Lebanese dining experience and serving fresh and exciting dishes at affordable prices across the north west.

Bakchich
HARISSA CHICKEN TAOUK

This recipe is one of my favourites. Not only is it easy to make, but the taste is out of this world. And if you like a kick, simply add more harissa paste! We think this dish pairs well with many great salads, a few helpings of rice and some delicious flat breads.

Preparation time: 20 minutes, plus 2-8 hours marinating | Cooking time: 15 minutes | Serves 4

Ingredients

4 chicken breasts

1 tbsp olive oil

2 tbsp natural yoghurt

4 tbsp lemon juice

1 tbsp red pepper paste

1 tsp harissa

2 tsp mixed spice

1 tsp salt

1 tsp black pepper

1 tomato, grated

Method

First slice the chicken breasts into cube shapes, then cover and place in the fridge while you make a start on the marinade.

In a medium bowl, combine the olive oil, yoghurt, lemon juice, red pepper paste, harissa, mixed spice, salt, black pepper and grated tomato.

Add the chicken to the marinade and mix well. Tip into a non-reactive container and refrigerate for 2-8 hours.

Next make the skewers, putting around four chunks of chicken on each.

Cook the chicken skewers on a hot grill for 15 minutes or until cooked through, making sure to rotate them regularly.

Serve with your favourite salad, rice and flat breads. Enjoy!

Food, drink and MUSIC

A creative vibe, well thought out food, local craft beer and Punk Afternoon Teas have put The Baltic Social on the Merseyside map.

"It's an alternative afternoon tea," says Alison Lockett-Burke, director of The Baltic Social. "That's our take on traditional afternoon tea."

She's referring to the venue's Punk Afternoon Tea, which replaces sandwiches and cakes with ingredients like hamburgers, ham hocks and mac and cheese, served with vintage teapots filled with Baltic Social beer or elderflower gin cocktails.

Alison said: "There's nothing better than watching groups of guys drinking beer from teacups enjoying afternoon tea as well as the more typical afternoon tea clientele. It seems to attract everybody which is great. People are intrigued by the idea of it being something a bit different."

Based in the ground floor of a Grade II listed warehouse in the Baltic Triangle area, with Elevator Studios above it, The Baltic Social opened in 2013. A mismatch of furniture, including reclaimed cinema seats, give a vintage look inside the bare brick walls.

The venue's known for its mixture of food, drink and regular live music. As well as the Punk Afternoon Tea, the menu is packed with well-crafted small plates, sandwiches, burgers and salads.

Alison said: "We've got a brilliant chef team – Andy and Miah, who are focusing on really good, simple, fresh food that's a bit more local as well."

Beer is a big part of The Baltic Social too, with independent brewers the main suppliers.

"We have a great craft beer selection that's always changing," said Alison.

"We're in the Liverpool 10 top craft beer pubs. Some kegs are just rolled down the hill because the brewers are that close."

The Baltic Social attracts a real mixture of people. With the recording studios above, it's not unusual to spot a famous musician, band or DJ, but families, friends and business people are all regulars too.

"When we got the idea together, it was always about it being a social place for everybody, and that's what we intend to create with the food and drink," said Alison.

"It's a home from home."

The Baltic Social
BLACK PUDDING AND CELERIAC REMOULADE WITH CHILLI OIL

A super brunch dish with the added benefit that the black pudding is homemade – it's easier than you may have thought.

Preparation time: 45 minutes plus overnight soaking | Cooking time: 1 hour | Serves 6

Ingredients

For the black pudding:

150g dried pig's blood (available to buy online)

200ml white wine vinegar

3l of beer

100g white sugar

500g back fat (suet)

500g white onion

500g barley, soaked overnight

5g salt

5g pepper

5g mace

10 sprigs thyme

Black pudding casing (available to buy online)

For the celeriac remoulade:

500g celeriac

350g crème fraiche

2 lemons, juiced and the zest from one of them

20g whole grain mustard

Salt and pepper

For the chilli oil:

150ml olive oil

3 large red chillis

Method

The easiest way is to have all of your ingredients weighed out before you start.

For the black pudding

Take the skin off the back fat and finely dice it, chop the thyme and dice the onion, then place into a pan and sweat on a low heat for 5-10 minutes. Try not to colour your onions, it will be ready when the fat is translucent.

Add the vinegar and sugar to the pan and cook on a high heat until reduced and like a thick syrup.

Meanwhile add the beer to the pig's blood, with plenty of salt and pepper, mace and the vinegar mix once it has cooled. Mix well. It should have a dough-like consistency.

Stuff the mix into black pudding casings and tie with butchers string. It needs to be really tight so no water can get in.

Submerge black pudding into a pan of cold water, making sure the pan is big enough to hold the black pudding and there is enough water to cover it. Bring to the boil and cook on a medium heat, simmer for 1 hour.

Cool and slice into thick rings. It's best to leave this for a few hours in the fridge before using.

For the remoulade

Finely grate the celeriac, then add all ingredients and mix well. Season to taste.

For the chilli oil

Take the heads off the chillis, slice them lengthways and remove seeds. Put in a pan with the olive oil, and cook on a low heat for 5 minutes. Remove from heat and once cool blend until smooth.

To serve

Fry the black pudding and serve with a portion of remoulade, drizzled with chilli oil. A fried egg also goes well with this dish.

The home of
SCOUSE

With a reputation for the best Scouse in Liverpool, its own microbrewery and a colourful history involving press gangs and ladies of the night, The Baltic Fleet is a Merseyside must-visit.

Scouse arrived in Liverpool – and at The Baltic Fleet – courtesy of the Scandinavian sailors involved in the international timber trade. The pub has been serving its own renowned version of the hot stew, which has its roots in the Norwegian dish lapskaus, for more than 160 years.

Scouse is on The Baltic Fleet lunchtime menu every day and the pub has won a well-deserved reputation for its version of the filling meal.

"Lots of people come in for the Scouse," said Baltic Fleet manager Richard Lee.

"We have a mixture of locals and tourists – and lots of Americans."

Scouse is served alongside other traditional quality pub food, including homemade steak and ale pies, chicken pies, ploughman's and burgers. They're dishes that go down well with the pub's home-brewed real ales made in its own microbrewery in the cellar. Summer Ale, The Baltic Fleet's year-round real beer, is also a key ingredient in the Scouse and the steak and ale pies.

"We've had the microbrewery since 2001 and we're now technically the oldest brewer in Liverpool since Cains closed," said Richard.

"Summer Ale is brewed all year round and we have seasonal brews as well."

In addition to its own beers, The Baltic Fleet champions other real ales and has earned the LocAle Pub of the Year accolade from CAMRA. There are usually around seven different cask ales available, all sourced from within a 10-mile radius of the pub.

Drinkers can also sample the 25 different gins, 25 whiskies and wide selection of rums available behind the bar in the jukebox and fruit machine-free pub, which encourages customers to chat and play bar games such as dominoes and cards.

Originally two buildings, The Baltic Fleet is a Grade II listed pub with a rich history involving Royal Navy press gangs, prostitutes and a former landlord who kept a set of handcuffs behind the bar to deal with unruly customers. There are tales of three ghosts who haunt the building, which is decked out in heritage colours, wooden floors and has a traditional mahogany bar. A wood burning stove keeps customers cosy in winter.

"At the front of the pub – the bow – are big, open windows," says Richard.

"There is lots of light and you can see some great sunsets over the Liver Building."

The Baltic Fleet
TRADITIONAL SCOUSE

Scouse is Liverpool's signature dish and this recipe, from the 'home of Scouse'
is as authentic as you'll get.

Preparation time: 15 minutes | Cooking time: 2-3 hours | Serves 4

Ingredients

4 tbsp oil

700g chuck steak, diced

2 bay leaves

1 sprig thyme

25g parsley, chopped

400g onion, diced

350g swede, peeled and cut into
2cm cubes

350g carrots, peeled and cut into
2cm cubes

600g potatoes, peeled and cut into
2cm cubes

500ml Baltic Summer Ale

1.2 litres beef stock

Salt and pepper

Method

Heat the oil in a large saucepan over a medium heat for about 1 minute.

Add the diced chuck steak and stir occasionally to prevent sticking. Cook until the meat is evenly browned on all sides, then season with salt and pepper.

Add the onions and cook until soft.

Add the Baltic Fleet Summer Ale and simmer until the liquid has reduced by half.

Add the diced and peeled carrot, swede and half of the potato, followed by bay leaves, thyme and parsley.

Then add in the beef stock, bring to the boil and simmer for 30 minutes.

Add in the rest of the potato and simmer for an hour and a half until the meat is tender. Check the seasoning and serve.

To garnish

At The Baltic Fleet our Scouse is served in the traditional way with pickled beetroot or pickled red cabbage, and chunky sliced white bread and butter.

From farm to FORK

Operating on the idea of quality above all else, Bexleys' experienced butchers source only the finest ethically produced cuts of meat.

Whether you are after award-winning sausages, well marinated meats or perfectly aged steaks, Bexleys are dedicated to providing exactly what the customer wants with an extraordinary level of freshness and quality. In order to consistently deliver outstanding meat, Bexleys assess farms within the British Isles that ethically raise and rear animals to the highest standards.

All suppliers have all gone through a thorough and rigorous vetting process to become an approved Bexleys supplier. They don't buy cuts, they buy whole carcasses for the team of expert butchers to treat, work and prepare the meat themselves, guaranteeing tender tasty cuts every single time. "If you want something done right, do it yourself. We care about what we serve our customers – we're involved in the process from farm to fork," says director Paul Brereton.

Bexleys have been leaders in making some of the most innovative traditional sausages over the last decade. They are freshly prepared daily and made using specially selected cuts of pork shoulder and belly which is cut and well trimmed by hand. The meat is then minced before the seasonings and ingredients are added to make them special and ready to be filled into natural skins and hand-linked the traditional way.

This gives them a lovely texture with a high meat content varying between 80%-95% meat.

Paul works incredibly closely with his clients, often offering specific cuts or bespoke treatments such as mature aged and cured meats. They pride themselves on the number of fine restaurants in the region they supply including Panoramic34 and many who have contributed to this book!

If feeling peckish, head into Bexleys' in-house deli serving on-the-go food ranging from artisanal sandwiches and sausage rolls to piping hot pies and baked goods – all freshly prepared with the same care and attention they give to all their other products. They also have a talented catering division who are able to serve platters, buffets and desserts for all occasions at affordable prices, you can be sure that quality is not compromised for economy.

Since opening their first store in 2005 they have gone on to open four more across Merseyside thanks to the loyal support of their customers and hard-working team. Bexleys has come on in leaps and bounds, exceeding expectations as one of the regions finest purveyors of quality fresh meats, buffet foods and corporate supply. But just don't just take our word for it – go see for yourself!

Bexleys SCOTCH EGGS

There are many speculations about the origin of the famous Scotch egg but there is one thing that we can all agree on – they are a must at any picnic. The trick is to get the egg yolk nice and oozy once you cut or bite into it.

Preparation time: 25 minutes plus 20 minutes cooling | Cooking time: 20 minutes | Serves 8

Ingredients

10 medium eggs

500g high-quality pork sausage meat

1 tsp thyme, chopped

1 tsp sage, chopped

1 tsp parsley, chopped

1 handful of chives, chopped

Salt and pepper

Plain flour, for dusting

50ml milk

125g breadcrumbs

Oil, for frying

Method

Preheat the oven to 190°c, or gas mark 5.

In a pan, cover 8 of the eggs with water and place over a high heat. Bring to the boil, setting a timer for 1 minute, 45 seconds just as the water begins to bubble. After this time has passed, immediately set the eggs to cool in a bowl of ice-cold water.

Next place the sausage meat in a bowl and add the thyme, sage, parsley, chives and 2 tablespoons of water. Season with salt and pepper before mixing thoroughly. Using your hands, mould the mixture into eight patties. If you're struggling with a sticky consistency, try wetting your hands with cold water. Place in the fridge to cool for around 20 minutes.

Once the eggs are cold, carefully peel off the shells. Gently enclose an egg in the centre of each patty. To ease the process, try flattening the sausage meat before forming it around the egg. Lightly press the edges to seal.

Take two separate bowls, tipping the breadcrumbs into one, and the flour into the other along with a little seasoning. Then beat the remaining two eggs in a third bowl, gradually stirring in the milk until smooth and pale yellow in colour.

Now roll each meat-covered egg first in the flour, then in the egg mixture and lastly in the breadcrumbs, making sure of an even coating.

To cook, heat a deep fat fryer to 190°c. Or if you don't have one to hand, fill a saucepan with oil deep enough to cover the eggs, and heat to the same temperature. Fry the Scotch eggs for 2 minutes each and until golden brown in colour. Remove them from the oil with a slotted spoon and place on a cooling rack, allowing the oil to drain off on to a baking tray beneath.

When all of the Scotch eggs have been fried, place the rack and tray in the oven for a further 10 minutes. These are best enjoyed with the yolk oozing, straight from the oven.

Backing the BISTRO

"I didn't have any ID so I just showed him how hard I find it to bend down and get back up again" is just one of the many hilarious tweets you'll find on these guys' Twitter feed.

After Chester restaurant Sticky Walnut launched an online crowdfunding campaign to get their new venture off the ground, they didn't expect such an overwhelming response. However between their loyal patrons and ever-growing band of Twitter followers, they far surpassed their target to open Heswall bistro Burnt Truffle and have since been inspired to go for a third endeavour; Hispi in Didsbury.

Owner Gary Usher was keen to bring their "friendly neighbourhood bistro" style to Heswall, however he wanted the restaurant to have its own identity, rather than be a carbon copy of Sticky Walnut, so all the menus are written by head chef, Michael Wong who changes it monthly dependent on the season and strives to utilise the Wirral and Merseyside produce.

Everything is made from scratch in-house, from their sourdough bread to their ice cream – there is a real emphasis on fresh seasonal food and they source a lot of their produce locally from Edge Butchers, Wirral Watercress, Claremont Farm, Liverpool Craft Beer and Wirral Gin.

Their style of service is much like their approach to cooking; unfussy and casual, yet professional and attentive. General manager Emma Underwood is a finalist for the Front of House award at the national Young British Foodie Awards, she said: "We tell our staff to imagine they're hosting a dinner party and to treat customers as if they were guests in their own home."

With dishes like squid ink tagliatelle with shellfish bisque and crabmeat adorning their menu, it's no surprise that they have already managed to bag themselves an AA rosette after being open for just over a year. Their most popular dish is the melt-in-your-mouth Jacobs Ladder, which is beef short ribs braised for 2-3 hours until tender then glazed in a jus for 20 minutes just before serving with watercress, onion purée and chunky truffle and Parmesan chips.

Burnt Truffle hosts regular guest chef nights, where a chef from another restaurant comes and cooks a specially crafted tasting menu matched with hand-selected wines supplied by local people. So far they have had the likes of Ben Spalding, Mark Poynton and Dan Doherty cooking up a storm.

Everyone is talking about Burnt Truffle and not just because of their tongue-in-cheek tweets, but because of the quality modern-European bistro food they bring to the table.

Burnt Truffle

BAKED YOGHURT WITH STRAWBERRIES & ELDERFLOWER GRANITA

Baked yoghurt is a traditional Bengali dessert called Bhapa Doi. Usually it's flavoured with cardamom and served in ramekins with raisins and toasted nuts like hazelnuts and pistachios – so we're pistachios as a garnish. The elderflower cordial can be substituted for Champagne, for a special occasion perhaps!

Preparation time: 20 minutes plus 4 hours freezing and chilling time | Cooking time: 30 minutes | Serves 4

Ingredients

For the granita:

1 gelatine leaf

250ml elderflower cordial

250ml water

1 lime, juiced

For the yoghurt:

1 vanilla pod

500g natural yoghurt

500g condensed milk

Sprinkle of Demerara sugar

For the garnish:

400g strawberries, halved and stalk removed

50g pistachios, chopped

Method

For the granita

Firstly, bloom the gelatine leaf in cold water for 2 minutes. Meanwhile, whisk together the elderflower cordial with the water and juice of one lime. Measure out 200ml of the solution and bring that to the boil. Squeeze out the water from the gelatine and add the bloomed gelatine to the boiling solution, whisking to dissolve. Strain this through a fine sieve back into the original elderflower mix, pour into a 2-litre container and chill in the freezer for about an hour. Once frozen, take a fork and scrape the surface of the ice to form the granita.

For the yoghurt

Split the vanilla pod lengthways and scrape the seeds out. Then whisk together the yoghurt, condensed milk and vanilla seeds. Transfer the mixture to a shallow baking tray or casserole dish, place in a bain-marie and bake at 120°c for 15-20 minutes until set. Leave in fridge to cool.

To assemble

Glaze the baked yoghurt by sprinkling a thin layer of Demerara sugar over the yoghurt and leave under a very hot grill until caramelised. Alternatively use a blowtorch for the same effect.

Place some strawberries around in a bowl, take 3 chunks of baked yoghurt and arrange on top. Take the granita and spoon around the bowl. Finally, sprinkle the pistachios over the dish.

On the MONEY

A breath of fresh air, an incomparable space and a hidden gem – Buyers Club feels as if you have stumbled upon a secret.

Buyers Club is co-founded by a line-up of key players from Liverpool's food, drink and music scene – Sam Tawil of Bold Street Coffee, Miles Falkingham of Camp & Furnace, Daniel Heffy and Michael Harrison of Secret Diners Club, and Andrew Hill of Abandon Silence. They all contribute to the venue in their own way making it one of the most exciting venues in Liverpool to open in recent years.

Located in what was the Old Picket building – a famous Liverpool music venue – good wine, good food and good service is at the forefront of this project. They wanted it to be a relaxed bar where people could socialise and unwind, somewhere that they'd actually want to go themselves – always the best starting point with any enterprise.

It is essentially a wine bar attached to an impressive outdoor garden, club space and restaurant – there's nothing else in the city like this. They have one of the best wine selections in Liverpool and this is thanks to Devin Stewart of R & H Fine Wines who is hugely involved and the wine buyer for the venue.

Choose from platters of meats and cheese, Sunday roasts, Scotch eggs, octopus and quality coffee. The huge and varied offering makes Buyers Club stand out from other restaurants in the city – one night you can come and enjoy a drink with a couple of small plates at the bar and the next you can be enjoying a six course fine dining menu in the dining room.

Buyers Club's menu is tailored to the seasons by their team of experiential and talented chefs, always making sure that they have the highest quality, local, seasonal produce to showcase in their dishes. "We pride ourselves on the quality of ingredients – and we've actually taken this one step further for our foraging dinners with the chefs heading out into the wild to forage ingredients themselves," says Daniel.

The team are continually looking to push the Liverpool food scene forward, so expect more foraging dinners, a 'VS' series which sees their chefs go head to head with another restaurant and lots more unique and unconventional fine dining dinners. There are also plans for an on-site bakery, these guys are a force to be reckoned with!

Buyers Club

SOUTHERN FRIED CHICKEN WITH CORNBREAD

This Buyers Club recipe puts a fresh, fine dining spin on the classic Southern fried chicken dish served with pickled watermelon, cornbread and sweetcorn purée. It's proven to be a real crowd pleaser and works a treat with maple syrup for those with a sweet tooth.

Preparation time: 50 minutes plus 2-3 hours pickling | Cooking time: 1 hour 25 minutes | Serves 4

Ingredients

For the pickled watermelon:

175ml white wine vinegar

45g sugar

250g watermelon, 2cm cubes

For the corn purée:

300g fresh corn

75g onion

1 garlic clove

250g butter

50ml water

For the cornbread:

175g self-raising flour

105g semolina flour

1tsp salt

60g sugar

240ml milk

1 egg

60g melted butter

75g fresh corn

For the Southern fried chicken:

100g plain flour

½ tsp nutmeg

1 tsp ground black pepper

1 tsp fine salt

½ tsp mustard seeds

½ tsp sesame seeds

100ml milk

2 chicken breast fillets

Vegetable oil, for frying

To serve:

Popcorn

Maple syrup

Crispy thyme

Method

For the pickled watermelon

In a pan, add the vinegar and sugar and bring to the boil – pour this into a bowl and allow this to cool down in the fridge.

Once cooled, add the cubed watermelon to the pickling liquor for 2-3 hours.

For the corn purée

First melt the butter in a heated pan and add the onion and garlic. Sweat down for three minutes. Next add the corn and cook on a low heat for 20 minutes.

After this has been cooked, add the mixture to a blender with water and blitz on high speed for eight minutes before passing through a sieve.

For the cornbread

Mix together the flour, semolina, salt and sugar in a bowl and with a separate bowl, whisk together the milk and egg.

Add the wet liquid into the flour mixture and mix with a wooden spoon until smooth. Then gently fold in the melted butter and fresh corn.

Pour the mixture into a loaf tin and bake at 175°c for 45 minutes until golden brown.

For the Southern fried chicken

In a bowl mix all the dry ingredients and set to one side with a separate bowl containing the milk.

Cut each chicken breast into five strips and pass these between the flour mix and milk three times.

Fry in vegetable oil at 180°c for 4 minutes.

To serve

Grab a plate and start with a thick slice of cornbread placed in the middle, spread a healthy amount of corn purée on top of this followed by chunks of the pickled watermelon and finally the Southern fried chicken.

For that extra touch, drizzle some maple syrup on top and garnish with popcorn and crispy thyme leaves.

Peruvian FLAVOURS

Chicha brings authentic Peruvian food to Liverpool in an exciting venue on Bold Street.

Based in the old RAN shop on Bold Street, Chicha Peruvian Street Kitchen opened its doors in summer 2016 as the latest venture from the Bistro Qui? Group, which has a number of eateries dotted around Liverpool city centre and the North West.

Chicha's head chef, Bart McHugh, says: "This is one of the most exciting concepts I've ever worked with. Peruvian food is packed with flavour and makes the most of fresh ingredients and seasonal produce. We wanted to bring a taste of Peru back from our travels and introduce it to the people of Liverpool.

"In Peru, flowers are often used in the presentation of traditional food – even in small street huts – and we keep this trend alive in Chicha so that our dishes look vibrant and colourful."

Peruvian cuisine is heavily influenced by its proximity to the Amazon rainforest.

Bart said: "When in Peru, there are lots of restaurants dedicated to Amazonian food and I was amazed and delighted by the flavours, preparation and ingredients used in the food."

As well as authentic Peruvian flavour, Chicha provides a unique and traditional setting to enjoy your meal. Hand-made vases and masks, bamboo balustrades, upholstered armchairs, heavy wooden tables and bespoke graffiti on the walls all add to the vibrant atmosphere which is typical of South America.

Hand-decorated sinks and ornate mirrors, imported from Peru specifically, are carefully selected finishing touches which further enhance the Chicha experience.

This combination of typically Peruvian décor and stunning traditional flavours are attracting Liverpool's diners who are keen to try something different and Chicha is proving to be something of a hit.

Traditional Peruvian plates such as Ceviche – raw fish marinated in lime and chilli – and Yukka potato chips, which are hugely popular in Peru, can be found on the exciting and varied menu alongside the lamb's belly.

Chicha
LAMB BELLY WITH PISTACHIO AND OREGANO STUFFING

Served with sweet potato purée and smoky tomatoes, this is a taste of Peru you can prepare at home.

Preparation time: 20 minutes | Cooking time: 3-4 hours | Serves 4

Ingredients

500g lamb belly

Red wine

Olive oil

Chopped herbs

Salt and pepper

For the stuffing:

100g sausage meat

20g fresh oregano

20g garlic purée

20g minced chilli

10g rosemary

50g pistachio nuts, crushed

5g cayenne pepper

1 tsp Tabasco sauce

10g caster sugar

10g smoked sea salt

For the smoked heirloom tomatoes:

2 heirloom tomatoes, halved

Cornish sea salt

1 sprig rosemary

1 cup apple wood chips (for smoking)

For the sweet potato purée:

2 sweet potatoes

A few cloves of garlic

Method

For the stuffing

Place all of the ingredients apart from the sausage meat into a food processor and blitz until paste-like. Fold the mix into the sausage meat.

For the lamb belly

Lay the 500g lamb belly flat, skin side down and sprinkle with chopped herbs and plenty of salt and pepper. Place the stuffing on top, roll over and tie up tightly.

In a hot heavy bottomed pan, add a splash of olive oil and brown the breast all over, seasoning as you go.

Transfer to a roasting tray, tip red wine over the lamb, then cover tightly with foil.

Cook gently in the oven for 3-4 hours.

For the sweet potato purée

Place the sweet potatoes on a foil lined pan with some garlic cloves. Bake for 45 minutes to an hour until tender. Then purée with salt in a food processor until smooth.

For the smoked heirloom tomatoes

Take a metal tray, chicken wire and wood chips (preferably hickory or beechwood). This will need to go on stove and be covered with tin foil to contain the smoke.

Add the salt and the rosemary to the halved tomatoes and place on the chicken wire above the wood chips. Smoke for 4-5 minutes.

Seeing STARS

A unique venue set in Liverpool's cultural quarter, Constellations and The Observatory is a space to eat, drink, and celebrate.

'A celebration of everything marginal, curious and inspired' is how Constellations & The Observatory sees itself.

Based in Liverpool's Baltic Triangle, it's a space for music, arts, culture and food – and also somewhere to relax with a great drink, grab a breakfast at the weekend Brunch Club, dine alfresco at their summer evening garden barbecues or attend a themed event, check out the website to see what events are coming up.

Opening in 2014 in a converted warehouse and recycling yard, visitors will find three different spaces – the award winning garden, the lobby bar and the observatory event Space. It provides people with spaces to gather whether that's for a private event such as a wedding or a gig, festival, exhibition, product launch, or a corporate event. Events are central to what Constellations is about.

The lobby-bar is open late and hosts intimate live music events throughout the week, serving bar snacks and drinks, including local craft beers and real ales. Weekend mornings are all about the Brunch Club, with a menu of simple quality food, specials and themes to the accompaniment of live music and DJs.

During the summer months, a barbecue is on the go in the garden from lunchtime until late. Throughout the winter many of the events are driven by food and Constellations often invites street food vendors to trade from the garden, providing a greater range of offers.

It's location in the Baltic Triangle, Liverpool's creative quarter, means the venue attracts plenty of artists, musicians, entrepreneurs, creatives and people working in the expanding tech sector. You'll find a diverse range of exhibitions on the walls in the Constellations lobby-bar, giving artists an opportunity to showcase and sell their work.

The design of the former warehouse is a work of art in itself. In 2015, the Garden Bar won a design award at the National Wood Award and was shortlisted for a Royal Institute of British Architects award.

Taking a trip to Constellations, whether you're popping in for a beer and burger or attending an event, is a real feast for the senses.

Constellations
EGGS BENEDICT

This perennial brunch favourite is made extra special with the addition of homemade hollandaise sauce.

Preparation time: 10 minutes | Cooking time: 15 minutes | Serves 4 (or 2 if you're hungry)

Ingredients

3 tbsp white wine vinegar

4 large free-range eggs

Hollandaise sauce (see below)

4 slices Parma or Serrano ham

50g rocket or spinach

2 English muffins

For the hollandaise sauce:

3 tbsp white wine vinegar

2 egg yolks

125g butter

Lemon juice

Salt and pepper

Bay leaf

½ tsp English mustard

Method

For the hollandaise sauce

Reduce the vinegar in a small pan with some peppercorns and a bay leaf over a high heat. When there is only 1 tbsp left, strain the peppercorns and remove bay leaf.

Pour the egg yolks and reduced vinegar into a food processor.

Place butter in a glass bowl over a boiling pan of water and gently melt the butter so that the salt solids fall to the bottom of the bowl.

With the food processor on low slowly pour in the butter on to the egg yolks. The sauce will start to thicken.

Season to taste with salt and pepper and a little lemon juice.

For the eggs Benedict

Boil 2 litres of water in a deep saucepan and add the vinegar. Crack the eggs into 4 separate ramekin cups and place to one side. Place the muffins in the toaster, and warm some plates in the oven.

Form a vortex swirling the water and slide in an egg. This helps the egg set to a nice shape by curling around itself. Cook for 2-3 minutes, then remove with a slotted spoon. Repeat this process with the other 3 eggs.

Place a small dollop of hollandaise sauce on each muffin, add a small amount of rocket or spinach, fold a slice of ham on top, and then top each muffin with an egg. Spoon over some hollandaise, sprinkle with black pepper and add pea shoots to garnish.

Constellations

HOMEMADE BAKED BEANS

There's nothing more comforting than a big pot of homemade baked beans on a cold day. Try this delicious and versatile recipe, and you won't want to eat the tinned version ever again.

Preparation time: Overnight | Cooking time: 3 hours | Serves 4 (or 2 if you're hungry)

Ingredients

100g dried haricot blanc, soaked overnight in cold water

100g borlotti beans, soaked overnight in cold water

100g tinned red kidney beans

100g tinned white kidney beans

60ml rapeseed oil

200g smoked streaky bacon, chopped (optional)

180g onion, finely chopped

2 garlic cloves, grated

800g tinned chopped tomatoes

2 tbsp tomato purée

150g soft dark brown sugar

200ml red wine vinegar

Sea salt and freshly ground black pepper

½ tbsp Marmite

¼ tsp English mustard

500g vegetable stock water

2 pinches of paprika

Method

Drain the haricot and borlotti beans and put them in a large pan full of water. Cover with water and bring to the boil.

Drain the beans again and return to the pan. Cover with water and cook until soft, around an hour. Remove from the heat and drain. Add the two different types of kidney beans to the mix at this point

Fry the onion and garlic in some rapeseed oil in a large pan and cook until the onion is soft (this is where you can add the smoked streaky bacon if you want to make it a meat dish). Add the tinned tomatoes, tomato purée, sugar, vinegar, two pinches of paprika, 500ml vegetable stock water, Marmite and English mustard. Boil and then add all the beans.

On a low heat, cook for 2 hours until the sauce is thick and the beans are tender.

Season the beans with salt and pepper and serve.

Constellations

A duo of refreshing drinks, one alcoholic and one non-alcoholic, that pair well
with the brunch recipes on the previous pages.

Preparation time: 3 minutes | Serves 1

Ingredients

For the fresh mint tea:

5-10 mint sprigs

1 mug hot water (about 350ml)

Honey/sugar/agave syrup to taste

For the bloody Mary:

½ lemon, juiced (about 30ml)

50ml vodka (we like to use Absolut)

125ml tomato juice

5 dashes Worcestershire sauce or
mushroom ketchup for a good vegan
alternative

2-5 dashes Tabasco (depending on
how spicy you like it)

Pinch of celery salt

Pinch of ground black pepper

To garnish:

A celery stick is traditionally used. If
you are feeling a bit extravagant and
have a hankering for meat to help
ease the hangover, a nice bit of crispy
bacon also works very well.

Method

For the fresh mint tea

Fresh mint works wonders in this very simple hot infusion, you can easily let it cool and
store it in the fridge to drink as iced tea on a hot day. In terms of flavour and quality there
is no comparing fresh mint tea to dried tea bags. Dried mint tea tends to become bitter
when over brewed, but there is no fear of over brewing fresh mint. If anything, the more
fresh mint brews, the more essential minty oils get released into the cup.

Take 5-10 mint sprigs, remove the leaves from approximately half of the stems and rip
roughly to help release the aroma and oils. Throw away the stems that have had leaves
removed from.

Place ripped leaves into the tall tea mug followed by the remaining stems with leaves still
intact. Pour in hot water from the kettle (mint is hardy and can take boiling water!).

Steep for 2-3 minutes before drinking. Add your choice of sweetener if you feel the drink
needs it (we like to use honey but sugar or agave syrup also work very well).

Once finished you can simply top up with more hot water for some more delicious minty
goodness.

For the bloody Mary

A bloody Mary is often referred to as "restorative" and consumed as a hangover cure. But
does it really work? Only one way to find out…

Add plenty of ice and all the ingredients to a shaker or stirring glass.

If using a shaker, tilt it backwards and forwards a few times to mix the ingredients without
making the drink frothy. If you are stirring you can do so quite vigorously.

Pour the mix into the serving glass (we like to use a hurricane glass but any tall glass will
do).

Garnish and enjoy!

Tips

Bloody Mary's are super versatile. The vodka could be substituted with gin to make it a
Red Snapper or tequila to make a Bloody Maria, or just leave out the alcohol to make a
Virgin Mary. You can also substitute the Tabasco sauce for wasabi or Sriracha hot sauce
for an Asian twist. A teaspoon of horseradish also works quite well.

Some people like to add a dash of red wine or port to give the drink a bit more of a boozy
kick. You should experiment to see what combination you like best.

From beans to
BREWING

Crosby Coffee take a lot of pride in what they do, from every hand stamped bag to each micro roasted batch of premium quality coffee.

Crosby Coffee was born from an obsession for coffee perfection by founder, Jack Foster. A Crosby born coffee fanatic who believed there was more of a story to coffee than meets the common eye. Jack started by roasting his own coffee at home as a hobby which soon developed into something more, he spent a year selling it to friends and family before deciding to take the leap and make it into an official business. In November 2014 Crosby Coffee moved into an industrial unit, which features a roastery and showroom in the back and serves specialty coffee and cake out front.

The unit is kitted out in pallets and reclaimed wood and has a very rustic look, customers come from all over since it became a destination for coffee lovers. They have gained a strong customer base and following through meeting customers needs and going beyond, whether it's bringing customers into the roastery for demonstrations or creating one-off bespoke blends for special events, wholesale customers and even weddings.

"We are young lads from the local area giving our dream a go. I know that it can be a struggle to get freshly roast coffee and that is why we roast weekly to order rather than mass producing and over-selling to our customers," says Jack.

Jack now predominantly supplies freshly roasted coffee and brewing equipment to restaurants, cafés and bars across the North West – they even go as far as London, Wales and Scotland! This is on top of selling online and attending a bunch of food festivals and markets. They recently supplied Aintree's Grand National 2016 where their coffee was used in the VIP areas and restaurants for guests to enjoy with their afternoon tea.

Their coffee is sourced from all over the country, either through suppliers or directly from farms in Brazil, Malawi and Guatemala. "Our most popular coffee is the Iron Men Crosby blend which was named after the Anthony Gormley statues on the beach. The tie with Crosby and the Iron Men has put our name and brand on the map in Liverpool," says Jack. Other crowd-pleasers are the coffee bean chocolate bars and espresso brownies, which were created in collaboration with The Macaron Lounge in Ainsdale village.

After being nominated for numerous awards; winning producer of the year at the Liverpool Food and Drink awards and featuring in the Northern Independent Coffee Guide for two consecutive years, Jack is looking to expand by opening two other coffee shops within the next year as well as expanding the roastery and showroom within the next two years.

Crosby Coffee
MOCHA BROWNIE

For this recipe we use our Ethiopian Yirgacheffe coffee, ground quite fine. We use this as it's a light roast, fruity and has loads of flavour. You could use something similar like Malawi Phoka or Colombia La Primavera.

Preparation time: 10 minutes, plus 5-10 minutes cooling | Cooking time: 35 minutes | Makes 16 Brownies

Ingredients

For the brownies:

225ml vegetable oil

375g white caster sugar

10ml vanilla extract

4 eggs

120g plain flour

30g cocoa powder

30g Ethiopian Yirgacheffe coffee, ground

2g baking powder

4g salt

For the ganache:

200g dark chocolate, 55% cocoa

100ml double cream

1 double shot espresso coffee

Method

For the brownies

Cream the eggs, sugar and vanilla with an electric mixer until the mixture has doubled in volume or until the batter falls slowly off the beaters, forming a ribbon that holds its shape for a few minutes. Slowly add the oil, being careful not to split the mixture.

Gently sift and fold in all the dry ingredients.

Pour the mixture onto a paper-lined tray and bake in the oven at 170°c for approx. 35 minutes.

Leave to stand for 5-10 minutes before devouring. We suggest a pairing with your favourite ice cream or if you're feeling confident, top your brownies with our smooth espresso ganache.

For the ganache

Melt the dark chocolate in a bowl over a pan of boiling water or, if you prefer, in the microwave making sure to stir consistently.

In a pan, boil the cream before pouring into the melted chocolate.

Add in the espresso coffee and mix well to form a smooth ganache.

Pour on top of the brownies and chill for 1 hour before serving.

Recipe for SUCCESS

A sprinkling of love, a dash of generosity – step into Cuthbert's Bakehouse, cornucopia of creativity.

Founders Matthew and Elaine Price developed Cuthbert's Bakehouse with the help of a scrapbook they compiled together through their love of travel and great food. They initially set up from their home back in 2006 and as the cakes continued to bake and orders continued to rise, their family home soon became a 24-hour bakehouse and it was time to expand to their very own premises.

Cuthbert's Bakehouse is now situated on one of the oldest streets in Liverpool, the building is hundreds of years old and funnily enough, it used to be a confectioners – they even still have the oven! It became the first tea room to open in Liverpool that sells and bakes everything on-site, however they now use local suppliers such as their local bagelry, French Corner and SourD-O for bread – this is so they can focus on making the best sweet treats and pastries.

Matt is a self-taught baker who draws a lot of his inspiration from New York; this is portrayed in their 'New Yorker' afternoon tea menu which features mini hot dogs, Reuben pastrami, cannoli and New York cheesecake. Other popular choices include their salted caramel brownies, red velvet cupcakes and their renowned velvety vanilla custard tart – Matt plans on taking this recipe to his grave!

A lot of thought and care has gone into the décor of the little bakery, from their daily specials inscribed on a huge scroll of parchment paper to their magnificent display of vintage china – Elaine's dad builds the tiered afternoon tea stands himself! They made it in the Top 25 Independent Afternoon Teas in the Independent newspaper last year and the lucky couple were also chosen to appear on television show Heston's Great British Food after researchers wanted to feature people who lived and breathed afternoon tea.

"It was the most amazing experience, we make so many afternoon teas but we never really get the opportunity to have it ourselves so getting to try one made by Heston Blumenthal was a real treat," says Elaine.

Expanding the premises is on the horizon for the future of Cuthbert's as well as the development of more gluten-free, dairy-free and vegan treats. Elaine is going to continue being the idea generator and Matthew's baking skills will be responsible for bringing them to life, the duo complement each other wonderfully which is a sure-fire recipe for success.

Cuthbert's
bakehouse

Thank You!
See You
Soon!

Cuthbert's
LIME & PISTACHIO DRIZZLE

The secret of our recipe is the hot, sticky syrup which is poured onto the cake when it's singing straight from the oven, giving it a lovely moist, Madeira-like texture. It's also a great cake to experiment with flavour: pistachio and lime are two ingredients which just aren't used enough in baking! – They complement each other perfectly, giving a lovely zingy, nutty taste.

Preparation time: 20 minutes | Cooking time: 50 minutes | Serves 10-12

Ingredients

For the cake:

300g softened butter

300g white caster sugar

3 limes, zested

100g pistachios, blitzed in a food processor – (keep a few aside to garnish!)

6 eggs

250g self-raising flour

1 tsp baking powder

For the drizzle:

50g white caster sugar

3 limes, juiced – (save a spoonful for the icing!)

For the icing:

300g fondant icing sugar

1 tbsp lime juice

4 tbsp water

Method

Preheat the oven to 160°c, or gas mark 3.

Grease and line a 20cm, round spring-form cake tin.

Beat the butter, sugar, lime zest and ground pistachios until pale and fluffy. If you are using an electric mixer, walk away for a while. The longer you leave it, the lighter the mixture and more voluminous the cake will be.

Turn off the mixer and carefully add the eggs, flour and baking power. Make sure the mix is properly combined before transferring into the cake tin.

Place the cake into the oven and bake for 50-55 minutes. My mam's tip for checking if a cake is ready is to listen and check 'if it's singing'. This little tip has saved me from many sunken cakes and soggy bottoms. If you can't hear the cake bubbling, pop it back in the oven for a few extra minutes.

To make the drizzle, tip 50g of caster sugar and the lime juice into a saucepan and bring to a simmer. If the limes aren't very juicy, you can add a touch of water. Once simmering, remove from the heat and place aside. Just re-heat once the cake is ready as it's important to pour over a hot drizzle.

Once the cake is ready, transfer onto a wire rack, spring open and remove the tin.

Re-heat the drizzle and gently pour over the warm cake before leaving to cool completely.

To finish, mix the retained tablespoon of lime juice and the water into the fondant icing sugar. The trick is to make sure it remains pourable, but not runny. Gently pour over the cooled cake, allowing it to drop over the sides.

To serve

Finish off with a sprinkling of pistachios and enjoy as a great afternoon treat.

Deli HEAVEN

Splice owner Candice Fonseca's surname with deli and you have Liverpool's independent award-winning foodie paradise Delifonseca Dockside.

"I've always been crazy about food," says Candice Fonseca.

Born in Hong Kong and growing up in Bury, Greater Manchester, with a father who was born in Shanghai, Candice's early adventures in food were very different to her schoolmates' and coloured her approach to eating. It's something that years later, she wove into the Delifonseca experience.

Candice said: "My dad cooked quite a lot and I grew up eating more rice and pasta than potatoes. Food was always central to the family. I grew up eating very well and definitely differently to a lot of my friends.

"Bury had a three days-a-week proper outdoor market, with a large number of stalls selling foods ranging from cheese to fruit and vegetable and with a fresh fish and meat market. When I was growing up, I thought this was normal."

Candice's career took her into TV and film and she worked in cities across the UK. She quickly realised that her 'normal' shopping, buying fresh, local and seasonal food was different to most people's experience of a trip to the supermarket. When she moved to Liverpool, the idea of opening a deli began to take shape.

"I saw a gap in market, and I could potentially see more people like me moving into the city needing food," said Candice.

"The provision in the centre – even the supermarkets – was poor. But I really dallied; it took about three years from the initial plans to going ahead with it."

In 2006, she opened the original Delifonseca in Stanley Street with the signature combination of retail deli with restaurant attached. The larger Delifonseca Dockside opened in 2010 at Brunswick Quay. With the additional space the deli blossomed into a food hall including an in-house butchers. Meanwhile the original deli space on Stanley Street was converted into the downstairs bar that is there today. The brand also has a busy outside catering division.

Delifonseca Dockside, which has on-site parking, is a flagship store for foodies with a great choice of local, regional and international produce: cheeses, charcuterie, antipasti, fruit, vegetables, beers, wines and spirits and meat from renowned Merseyside butchers Edge & Son. Takeaway lunches are also available.

A trip to Delifonseca Dockside is all about being enthused about food. The staff share Candice's passion for eating well and can offer advice and guidance to shoppers.

Candice said: "We're a business but that's kind of secondary – it's about doing something you believe in and believe should exist. Producers need an outlet to show people how good things can taste when they're done with passion and with respect for the environment and animals involved."

EDGE & SON BUTCHERS

Delifonseca Dockside

CHEESEBOARD SELECTION:

LIVERPOOL GIN ROSE

EDGE & SON BUTCHERS

delifonseca
foodhall butcher eatery

Dining at
DELIFONESCA

Delifonesca and Fonseca's are famed for their blackboard menu of ever-changing dishes making the most of fresh, seasonal ingredients.

Dining is a real celebration in seasonal eating. The blackboard consists of 12-14 main meals with new dishes appearing each day providing something fresh to discover every time.

"Our ever-changing blackboard menu is our signature," says Candice.

"It turns customers into regulars as they know there will be new dishes to try each time they come in."

"And it works well with the kitchen as creative freedom leads to happy chefs. They can work with whatever is in season or on trend."

Martin Cooper, who has been head chef since the business opened 10 years ago and current head chef Marc Lara share Candice's philosophy. The menu reflects what's good to eat, right now. Diners will find a great choice of modern takes on traditional British favourites and global dishes. All made with the best of ingredients most of which can be purchased in the deli, whether they're popping in for breakfast, lunch or a three-course evening meal.

Deli platters are popular as shared starters. The deli dip platter includes mouth-watering in-house hummus, tahini and roasted red pepper and roasted aubergine pâté, whilst the Great British Platter showcases hand-raised pork and apple pie, rare Welsh black beef, roast deli ham and Mrs Kirkham's tasty Lancashire cheese. All elements are available for purchase from the food hall should the customers want to continue enjoying the taste at home.

Candice said: "It showcases the quality of our products and there's a crossover that encourages people to try things at home."

That extends to the wines available to buy in the Dockside shop, which can be enjoyed with your meal.

Candice said: "Often restaurant mark-ups can be high especially on more expensive wines. Instead what we do here is charge corkage of £6.50 for each bottle purchased from our deli and enjoyed in the restaurant. It's really good value, especially on the pricier wines. It means the customer has a much wider choice and has the option to buy more to drink at home too. Many of the staff are confident so can assist with finding the perfect wine for the meal."

Across at Fonseca's Stanley Street, the GM Danielle Youds is equally passionate about food and wine and uses the 'Downstairs Bar' regularly to host wine, beer and spirit evenings. These events give guests the chance to meet producers and enjoy a whole array of new drinks paired with great food. Having hosted wine producers from Australia or mixologists from Chase Distillery, the Downstairs Bar has also been used for alternative entertainments such as Cookbook Club or Murder Mystery evenings – but always with great food involved.

Upstairs the signature blackboard still dominates the original restaurant. It's complemented by another Fonseca innovation; the Wine or Fizz Flight. They have a high tech wine preservation system that means Fonseca's has a huge wine by the glass range.

Delifonseca

ROASTED RACK OF HEBRIDEAN MUTTON WITH STUFFED CURRIED VEGETABLES AND AN OLIVE JUS

This is one of our favourite dishes with it's big, bold flavours and eye-catching plating style. Take care to prep the vegetables correctly, it will mean the final dish has that restaurant quality finish.

Preparation time: 40 minutes plus 1 – 2hrs for sauce reduction | Cooking time: 40 minutes | Serves 6

Ingredients

1 rack of mutton (6 cutlets)

800g mutton mince

6 patty pan squash

1 jar artichoke hearts

6 strips of air-dried ham (e.g. Serrano..)

2 yellow courgettes, medium

1 green courgette, small

2 waxy potatoes, large (e.g Charlotte)

6 vine tomatoes

1 red onion

Handful of chopped chives (reserve some for garnish)

1 tsp curry powder

1 lemon

10 sprigs thyme

600ml lamb stock

½ bottle red wine

1 head garlic

100g chopped Kalamata olives

Butter

Olive Oil

Method

For the mutton

Trim and clean the rack of mutton, score the fat and keep the trim (your butcher should assist)

For the sauce

Place all the trim on a tray with the garlic and roast until golden brown. Remove from the oven, discard the excess fat and place the contents into a deep pan. Add the red wine and thyme, bring to boil then drop to simmer until the liquid is reduced by half. Add the stock and continue simmering until reduced by half again or until the sauce is thick enough to coat the back of a spoon.

For the vegetables

Finely dice the green courgette and red onion. Gently fry in butter until softened, remove from the heat.

Once cooled, mix with minced mutton, season with salt and pepper, add curry powder and chopped chives. Fry a small amount to check it is seasoned correctly.

Peel the potatoes and cut into three thick slices (approximately 1½ inch thick) Shape into a circle and scoop out the centre with a melon baller.

Carefully cut the first inch off the top of each patty pan and tomato. Cut the yellow courgettes into three pieces. Using a melon baller, gently scoop out the inside of each vegetable leaving a lip at the top. Season with salt and pepper then drizzle with olive oil.

For the mutton

Heat up a heavy bottomed pan and colour the mutton fat-side first. Once golden, place in preheated oven (180°c for approximately 20 minutes.) Remove and rest for 10 minutes, wrapped in tin foil.

As soon as the mutton is in the oven, also add a baking tray containing the patty pan, potatoes and yellow courgettes and bake for 10 minutes.

During that 10 minutes stuff the tomatoes and artichokes with the mince mix and wrap the artichokes in air-dried ham.

Once the 10 minutes is up, quickly remove the vegetables from the oven and spoon in the mutton mince to the vegetables. Add the stuffed tomatoes and artichokes to the tray and place back in the oven for a further 15-20 minutes. Keep an eye on your clock but if you've been quick stuffing your vegetables then after a further 5 minutes your rack of mutton will be ready to be taken out to rest whilst your vegetables are finishing up.

To serve

Arrange the vegetables upright around each plate. Slice the mutton into cutlets for the centre. Add the olives to the warm sauce and spoon over. Garnish with chives or pea shoots.

A day to REMEMBER

Located on Liverpool's iconic Water Street, District House marks the start of a new chapter for this part of the city.

Opening its doors in 2016, District House was created with the needs and tastes of the local people in mind – with the aim to provide an ideal and flexible space that can be used for multiple purposes. Whether it's a place for brunch, a drink after work or a stunning location for a private event, District House can provide the space and hospitality for any occasion day or night.

With many different options on the breakfast, lunch and dinner menus, including plenty for those with specific dietary requirements, there is no doubt that you will find something that suits your needs. Considerably tasty palate teasers include the smoked salmon ballotine, stuffed with crab, caviar and cream cheese, and the seared tuna niçoise salad tossed with green beans, diced potatoes and a poached egg.

The cocktail bar and lounge, Coffee & Liquor, serves everything from your morning caffeine fix through to brunch and afternoon tea. This venue brings a taste of the exotic to the heart of Liverpool, serving artisan coffee from local roastery Neighbourhood Coffee. The beans are delivered within days of roasting to give you the most delicious cup of coffee the city has to offer.

A selection of loose leaf teas and infusions are supplied by Phom on Hanover Street but if you fancy something stronger, they have a cleverly crafted cocktail menu which has been developed by bar guru Si Taylor. It has been designed to offer guests a unique range of simple balanced serves, created with premium spirit brands and homemade syrups.

Its also worth keeping an eye on the upcoming events at District House; maybe join a meditation class or have a meander through their mid-morning market showcasing some of the best independent market traders. Thanks to the fact that all tastes are catered for and the event space is so flexible, there are choices for every occasion – from a quiet afternoon tea to an important corporate event.

They can also provide a range of live entertainment and their exclusive VIP mezzanine for a range of private dining options – perfect for shaping the event into something really special.

From fantastic food and drinks to live music and entertainment, it's all waiting for you at District House.

District House

District House
EGGS BENEDICT

This classic breakfast dish is still super popular but you'd be surprised how many people struggle to make a decent hollandaise. The trick is to make sure you heat the sabayon and the whisk the butter in gradually to stop the eggs scrambling.

Cooking time: 10-15 minutes | Serves 6

Ingredients

12 eggs

6 English muffins

Splash of white wine vinegar

12 slices of ham

For the hollandaise sauce:

4 egg yolks, whisked

140g butter, melted

15ml white wine vinegar

4g salt

Pinch of black pepper

½ lemon

Method

To start with, sabayon the egg yolks, vinegar and salt by placing the ingredients in a metal bowl over boiling water and whisking constantly. Don't over fill the pan with water – too much heat will scramble the eggs.

Once the mix has started to thicken it should start to increase in volume so start to whisk in the melted butter slowly over the hot water for around 4-5 minutes or until all the butter has melted into the sauce. Take off the heat and add salt, pepper and freely-squeezed lemon to season. Put to one side.

To poach your eggs, boil a pan of water with a splash of white wine vinegar. Add two eggs and leave for 2½ minutes. Meanwhile, toast the muffins and put the sliced ham under the grill to take the chill off of them.

Take the eggs out of the pan and place on a sheet of kitchen roll; this should remove the excess water. Serve.

Elite meat for EVERYONE

With a shop on the Wirral and an outlet at Delifonseca, award-winning Edge & Son has been supplying Scousers with traditionally reared and butchered meat since Victorian times.

Introduced to Prince Charles as 'the best rare breed butcher in the country', Callum Edge is the sixth generation of his family to head up Edge & Son.

The shop has been trading from New Ferry beside Port Sunlight since 1844, and since the start of 2016, there's been an Edge & Son outlet at Delifonseca's Dockside food hall.

The ethos is the same at both sites: meat from local rare or traditionally-bred grass-fed stock sourced from within a 25-mile radius, which has been reared with respect on a proper farm and not a factory. Animals are killed and butchered at Edge's own slaughterhouse and the firm's own cutting room.

Customers can gain a thorough insight into the process at the Wirral shop and at Delifonesca, where carcasses are on show in a maturing fridge.

Callum's enthusiasm is also shared at Edge & Son's regular butchery masterclass sessions.

He said: "They've been running for more than 12 years. They're very popular with foodies and next week we have one for a mother, her two daughters and son. They started when we were approached to do a class for a customer's father for his 70th birthday."

Callum's wife Debbie, who works full-time in the business after a career in HR, has also developed the Butcher's Wife range in collaboration with a chef, to give shoppers ideas for using meat in new creative ways.

Cooks and chefs alike say that meat from native breeds farmed, killed and butchered properly really is different in flavour and texture; "it looks and tastes like meat used to be"; "the difference between chipboard and Chippendale"; "it tastes like another species it is so markedly different."

Edge & Son's championing of traditional butchery and traditionally reared stock has been recognised with awards from the RSPCA, and the shop has also won the best UK independent retailer at the BBC Food Awards. Callum was also a panel member and invited to speak at the Rare Breed Survival Trust conference at Prince Charles' home, Highgrove.

"Prince Charles spent a lot of time with us and he was really interested in what we do," said Callum.

But Edge & Son isn't a 'posh' butcher. Callum's philosophy is that good, natural food should be available to all.

He said: "New Ferry is not an affluent area but we are selling the best meat money can buy, and I'm really proud we're doing that. Good food must be available for everybody. I don't want it to be elitist."

Edge & Son
TEA SMOKED LAMB

This is sensationally easy and never fails to wow. It goes brilliantly with local spuds, seasonal green vegetables and hollandaise sauce.

Preparation time: 5 minutes plus 2-4 hours marinating time | Cooking time: 45-60 minutes | Serves 6-8

Ingredients

1 butterflied leg of Edge & Son Black faced Suffolk Lamb

4 tbsp fish sauce (optional – to marinate lamb for a few hours before cooking)

1 packet Edge & Son tea smoke mixture or make your own by mixing 2 cups rice; approx. 20 emptied teabags or the equivalent in loose tea; 1 cup sugar and 6 star anise.

Salt and pepper to season (no need to salt if fish sauce marinade has been used)

You will need a kettle barbeque or the equivalent for an outside closed oven heated to 180°c.

Method

Line a roasting tin with foil to cover all the sides and bottom. Put the tea smoke mixture in the foil lined roasting tin.

Place a roasting rack or equivalent in the roasting tin to put the lamb on and keep a distance between the tea smoke mixture and the meat.

When you are ready to cook, place your marinated or seasoned lamb on top of the rack.

Place the lamb in the preheated barbeque and close the lid. Roast it quickly for 20-25 minutes per pound depending on how pink you like it. This would take 60 minutes for a 3 lb leg of lamb served medium rare, longer for a little less pink.

It is useful to use a meat thermometer (sold in-store): the internal temperature should be 54-60°c for medium rare, 60-66°c for medium and 66-74°c for well done. The thermometer is king – if it says the meat is at the desired temperature, take it out and leave to rest.

Rest for 15-30 minutes, it will keep and improve well under the foil.

The smoke mixture in the bottom of the tray after cooking looks revolting. You will see why we line the tin with foil – bin it!

This method of smoking is fabulous with any meat at any time of year. We once smoked our Christmas turkey – great to have more space indoors for all the other bits and pieces and gives other family members a project to be in charge of on the day.

We change the smoke mixture approximately every hour of cooking time.

To serve

Serve with potatoes, seasonal vegetables and hollandaise sauce.

Interactive EATING

Fazenda takes social dining to a new level with its interactive take on sharing traditional Brazilian slow-roasted meat in a buzzing, friendly atmosphere.

A restaurant where the experience is almost as important as the delicious food on offer is what you're promised when you pay a trip to Fazenda.

This Brazilian restaurant serves a huge selection of meats, grilled slowly and brought to the table by passadores, in a buzzing atmosphere where everyone's welcome. It's all inspired by a rich slice of South American heritage.

"In the 19th century, gaúchos – or cowboys – travelled across South America herding their cattle," says Fazenda Liverpool's Business Development Manager, Dayle O'Hara.

"They would dig a big pit in the ground and slowly cook a large piece of beef, for example over the fire. Gathered around the fire, they would drink wine, tell stories, sing songs and slice off pieces of meat. This social way of eating epitomises the traditions of the gaúchos and the importance of sharing."

Fazenda mirrors this social tradition but with a totally modern take. Guests begin their journey at the gourmet sides bar, where there is an extensive selection of dishes such as cured meats, sushi and traditional Brazilian dishes such as Feijoada.

Dayle said: "Once guests have returned from the gourmet sides bar, they can turn their service control card to green, which indicates to our passadores that they are ready for their meat to be served. This is when the 'rodizio' (meaning 'to rotate') commences! With continuous tableside service, guests are able to have a rest in between cuts, even requesting particular meats that they may not have tried, or simply their favourite cut! This is the real beauty of concept."

Guests can choose up to eight cuts of meat at lunchtime and fifteen in the evening, cooked to their own taste! Cuts of beef include picanha (cap of rump), their signature cut which is juicy and full of flavour, melts in the mouth and is very popular in the churrascarias of Southern Brazil. Or there's the tri-tip or bottom sirloin, which is beautifully marbled and has superb flavour and texture.

They also serve the Cordeiro, a tender leg of lamb and gently flavoured with a fresh mint marinade, or for those of a more experimental nature – coração de frango. A firm favourite at Fazenda amongst the team, the corações de frango (chicken hearts) are an acquired taste but incredibly tender and juicy.

Just like the food, the décor also takes the style of the gaúchos and brings it up to date with a modern twist. Heavily influenced by the rodizios in São Paulo, Fazenda has a high end but rustic, homely feel with low lighting from suspended lamps to stucco walls adorned with saddles, all to enhance that gaúcho vibe.

It's an approach that has gone down a storm in Liverpool, both with locals and visitors to the city since Fazenda opened in 2013. It's been so good, in fact, that the restaurant has never moved out of the top 10 restaurants on TripAdvisor out of over 1, 400 restaurants in the city.

Dayle said: "We have a real mixture of guests visiting us. We're extremely popular with corporates visiting the city for conferences and with Liverpool having so much on offer with regard to culture, history and world class events, there are a lot of domestic and international tourists who come to visit us."

"A lot of our team are from Brazil, Argentina, Portugal, Spain and Italy and they have that connection with the tourists who come in. Having such a culturally diverse team really adds to our guests' experience here, whether local or international."

"Liverpool is a great city because of its up and coming dining scene. Liverpool as a city is renowned for its sense of community, which is built on interaction and sociability – and that's the concept at Fazenda."

Part of a small group that also has restaurants in Leeds and Manchester, Fazenda is not just about the food. With a driven passion for wine, it showcases a carefully selected wine list; a key ingredient for the Fazenda experience. From old world to new world styles, inclusive of a comprehensive selection of Argentinian and Brazilian wines, there is an offer for all palates. A temperature controlled wine room houses Fazenda's highly exclusive list, with extensively trained and knowledgeable staff at hand who can advise on the best wines to accompany your dishes and to suit your preferences.

Dayle says, "We're equally as passionate about serving quality wines as well as quality meats to our guests. We want to give them a completely unique dining experience like no other – something unforgettable"

Fazenda
PICANHA, VANILLA PANZANELLA & ROASTED GARLIC SAUCE

An authentic taste of South America with a cut of steak that's popular in Brazil, cooked in smoky paprika and served with a vanilla-infused salad and rich garlic sauce.

Preparation time: Overnight plus an hour | Cooking time: 1 hour 15 minutes | Serves 1

Ingredients

For the steak:

225g Picanha steak (cap of rump) or fillet steak.

50g smoked paprika

For the panzanella salad:

1 vanilla pod

50g extra virgin olive oil

10g white wine vinegar

3 heirloom tomatoes, mixed

¼ cucumber, peeled

2g sea salt flakes

For the roast garlic aioli:

1 bulb garlic

3 egg yolks

1g salt

50g extra virgin olive oil

Method

For the steak

Season the meat with the paprika, ensuring it's rubbed into both sides. Leave to marinate overnight in the fridge in cling film.

Take the meat out of the fridge 1 hour prior to cooking to bring it to room temperature. This will improve the tenderness of the steak.

For the garlic aioli

Cut off the top of the garlic head, place it on a piece of foil and drizzle with a dash of olive oil, wrapping the foil tightly to form a packet. Place on a tray and bake for about 45 minutes at 200°c.

Remove from the oven and rest until it is cool enough to handle, then squeeze the cloves into a bowl and add the egg yolks.

Place the garlic cloves and egg yolks into a food processor until the ingredients are combined (approximately 10 seconds) and with the processor slowly running, add the rest of the olive oil in a thin stream and process for a further 2 minutes.

Add the salt and blend for a few more seconds. You can prepare the aioli in advance and keep in the fridge for 3 days to achieve the maximum flavour in the sauce.

For the panzanella salad

Make the dressing by combining the olive oil, vinegar and the seeds from the vanilla bean in a small ramekin and leave it to infuse while preparing your vegetables.

Slice the tomato very thinly, dice the cucumber and dress with the vanilla vinaigrette on the plate. Season with salt flakes.

Steak cooking tips

The following is a few tips on how to cook a steak at home without all of the modern equipment that restaurants use. Preheat the oven to 160°c and using a cast iron griddle pan, place it over a high heat on the hob to sear the steak on both sides. At this point, the paprika rub plays a big role as we are looking to literally burn the spices and create a crust that will keep our meat juicier than ever, resembling a real smoky barbecue.

Next place the pan into the oven and finish to your liking. We would recommend approximately 20 minutes for medium-rare or until the temperature in the centre of the steak reaches 55°c when probed. Leave the steak to rest for a few minutes then slice across the grain and season with salt flakes.

Cuban KITCHEN

FINCA is the tale of four friends who all share a passion for food and wanted to serve up authentic Cuban fare to the people of Liverpool.

Michael Harrison, Daniel Heffy, Oli Smith and Joe Earnshaw all share the same passion – food.

When they were offered a space at the Botanical Gin Garden for the summer of 2016, they knew it was too good an opportunity to pass up – ergo Cuban street food restaurant FINCA was born.

From the pickles and marinades to the sauces and syrups, each and every item that FINCA serves is made fresh on-site, using the best local ingredients, which you can taste in each one of their delicious street-eats.

The legendary Cubano is a firm favourite with their loyal followers – a traditional Cuban sandwich that consists of pork shoulder marinated in homemade mojo sauce, glazed horseshoe gammon, pickles, mustard and Gouda. Their crispy plantain crisps and their sweet potato fries coated in a secret seasoning and topped with sour cream and chilli are also extremely popular with Liverpool foodies.

"We're constantly adding one-off specials to the menu. Lots of our items start as one-offs and then become permanent fixtures as customers enjoy them so much they won't let us take them off the menu – this happened with our croquettas." says Oli.

With their inaugural summer residency at the Botanical Gin Garden going down a storm, the lads have now brought their famous corrugated sign and Cuban shutters over to the kitchen at The Merchant, where they'll continue to serve up a taste of Havana – including the debut of their unique Cubano and lobster night.

In Cuba, a number of private restaurants from people's homes have been launched called Paladares where you literally dine in the homeowner's front room or at their kitchen table – one of the most vivid and best ways to enjoy local cuisine. Keep your eyes peeled for FINCA's own paladares which will take place in secret locations across Liverpool.

Expect to see a lot more of the rustic FINCA shack in the upcoming months, they'll soon be on the road sharing the Cuban love at festivals and events around the country, a trip to Cuba is on the cards (for research purposes obviously) and there are also talks of a permanent residence – one things for sure, FINCA and these four lads have a big future ahead.

Worth the WAIT

Michelin-starred chef Marc Wilkinson opened Fraiche to create a modern dining experience in a top-shelf restaurant – I defy you not to be impressed by his food.

Fraiche sits on a quiet suburban street in the pretty conservation village of Oxton, the discreet and understated façade leads you into an intimate space created with a theme of natural elements inspired by the shoreline reflecting nature. It's run by chef patron Marc Wilkinson who is aided by just one man in the kitchen.

Marc and the team strive to create a relaxed and less formal approach to service offering guests a warm welcome and a personal touch, while giving a professional and unobtrusive experience. The emphasis is always on guest enjoyment and comfort, from the well-spaced and uncluttered tables to carefully chosen music, lighting and visual displays – all under the direction of Marc. Not only does he champion local food suppliers, he also displays wall art from local artists Jenny Barker, Charlie MacPherson and Simon Smith.

Each season offers a subtle guideline to give Marc direction and inspiration, drawing out the finest ingredients and nuances that reinforce the seasons, which is translated through his modern progressive cuisine. The dishes are ever evolving; creative routes and modern approaches' open new doors to capturing exciting tastes and textures, which are involved in all menus.

"Fraiche is a very personal journey for me, building a modern cuisine on a classical trained foundation to keep my sensibilities in check. My expanding cooking techniques and cutting edge preparations help me to express myself, thus enabling me to offer our guests a complete experience, taking them on a both a culinary and visual journey. The drive is very much to push Fraiche to higher levels of cuisine for the enjoyment for our guests," says Marc.

They were awarded a Michelin star back in January 2009 which has been retained ever since. They have also gone on to win numerous awards over the years, including being named number one restaurant in the UK by the Sunday Times in 2014 alongside 4 AA rosettes and an amazing top 10 placing in the UK from the Good Food Guide 2017.

Michelin-starred chef Marc keeps his restaurant small to keep standards breathtakingly high. If you want a table at the tiny Oxton restaurant, note that they cater for around 12 diners a night and they are booked three months in advance, the bookings open at 10am on the 1st of each month for each 3 month period ahead – definitely worth the wait though.

Fraiche ROSEMARY

A luxurious and innovative dessert created by Marc Wilkinson – it's full of interesting flavours and textures and is sure to be a talking point at any dinner party!

Preparation time: 40 minutes plus 1-2 hours marinating and 1 hour chilling
Cooking time: 40 minutes | Serves 4/6

Ingredients

For the rosemary ice cream:

250ml milk

250ml double cream

1 tsp of rosemary, gently crushed to release the oils

6 free-range egg yolks

100g caster sugar

For the sesame crisp:

30g unsalted butter

65g caster sugar

35g plain flour

3 tsp black sesame seeds

25ml orange juice

1 tbsp carbon powder, not essential just to create the black colour

For the apple ribbon:

1 apple

100ml apple juice

½ tsp rose water

1 tsp grenadine

For the crumb:

150g plain flour

85g brown sugar

Pinch of cinnamon

Pinch of salt

100g unsalted butter, room temperature

Method

For the rosemary ice cream

For the ice cream, mix the milk and cream together in a saucepan and heat it up along with the rosemary, after it reaches 90°c take off the heat and cover, leaving the cream mixture to infuse for about 35 minutes. Once done, pass the cream mix through a sieve and put to one side.

Whisk the egg yolks and caster sugar together until it reaches the ribbon stage. Slowly whisk in the cream mix before gently heating up in a pan whilst stirring continuously. Do this until the mixture coats the back of a spoon and you can draw a line through the ice cream mixture.

Pass through a fine sieve once again to capture any lumps. Cool as quickly as you can before churning in an ice cream machine.

For the sesame crisp

Cream the softened butter and sugar together until creamy and smooth, add the flour and mix well before adding the orange juice and carbon powder. Once smooth, mix in the black sesame seeds and rest the mixture in a fridge for at least an hour.

Spread on a non-stick baking sheet and bake at 160°c for around 6-7 minutes. Allow to cool before transferring to an airtight container ready to use.

For the apple ribbon

Peel the apple and carefully create a ribbon with a potato peeler. Marinate the peel in apple juice, rose water and grenadine for 1-2 hours to create a floral rose effect

For the crumb

Mix the flour, sugar, cinnamon and salt together in a large bowl. Add the butter and rub into the mix using your fingertips to create the crumbs. Rest in the fridge until they resemble firm crumble pieces before baking on a non-stick sheet until golden brown and crisp at 160°c.

To assemble

Spoon the crumbs into a bowl, scoop the ice cream on top, garnish with the sesame crisp and place your marinated apple coiled to resemble a rose on top. If possible present your rose with mint or lemon balm leaves to finish the dish.

More than just BURGERS

Free State Kitchen is all about serving a contemporary twist on American classics, with quality, locally sourced produce at the heart of their menu.

Husband and wife team Kate Hughes and Gary Williams have always had the dream of opening their own restaurant; they were both coming up to the age of 30 and just thought: "You know what? It's time to do something for ourselves." The dynamic duo travelled America extensively in their twenties and together they decided to open an East Coast inspired restaurant serving American classics – thus Free State Kitchen was born.

The diner caters for everyone from babies right the way through to pensioners; people from all walks of life come to try their contemporary style food in an informal and fast-paced environment. "It's not just about the food; it's about the whole relaxed atmosphere and social aspect of it. We didn't want to replicate the traditional American diner, just the atmosphere." says Kate.

Everything in-house is made from scratch including their pickles and sauces, and a lot of their dishes feature ingredients from their own garden. In the warmer months there is another dimension to the restaurant in the form of a beautiful green space. The garden provides an attractive outdoor dining area and hosts a monthly Sunday market from April to

October. Fruit and vegetables are also grown including apples, strawberries, rhubarb, blackcurrants, pumpkins and herbs. These often provide the focus for the chef salad that is always on the specials board.

Free State Kitchen are big on supporting local businesses too, some of their favourites are The French Corner, Bexleys Butchers and Jess Turner which is where they get their bread, meat and potatoes from respectively. Vegetarians, gluten-free eaters and vegans are not forgotten with plenty of options on both their main menu and specials board which changes every 2-3 weeks. This is also their playground for experimenting with different trends; they recently collaborated with someone who makes kimchi (fermented Korean cabbage) nearby and incorporated this into their menu by serving kimchi hot dogs!

Everyone knows Free State Kitchen for their burgers; not dirty burgers, but classic burgers made with top quality produce and traditional American dressings. However their other options deserve some of the limelight too. Their Boston clam chowder is a hit and you can find the recipe overleaf along with their double French onion burger which won Liverpool's best burger in 2013.

Free State Kitchen

DOUBLE FRENCH ONION BURGER

This burger is considered to be the best we do. While most of the burgers we do at Free State Kitchen are classically American, this is a classy affair. It transports the sumptuous flavour of a rich French onion soup into a burger. Originally the burger was only part of the specials board, but our customers quickly forced us to put it on the menu full time.

Preparation time: 1 hour | Cooking time: 4-8 minutes | Serves 4

Ingredients

2 large onions

1 knob of butter

1 tsp vegetable oil

1.2kg good-quality ground beef, preferably ground chuck steak

Swiss cheese, sliced

4 good-quality brioche burger buns

Salt

For the garlic butter:

150g salted butter, at room temperature

1 large handful of flat leaf parsley, stalks retained and roughly chopped

1 tsp of salt

6 garlic cloves

For the Dijon mayonnaise:

3 tbsp good-quality mayonnaise

3 tbsp Dijon mustard

Method

Finely slice the onions and add to a heavy bottom frying pan, along with a knob of butter and teaspoon of vegetable oil. Cover and cook at a very low temperature for 30-45 minutes until nicely browned, sticky and caramelised. Remove the lid and place the pan to one side.

For the garlic butter

Peel and roughly chop the garlic cloves before gently frying in vegetable oil for 5-10 minutes. It wants to be softened without darkening in colour. Using cooked rather than raw garlic will help eliminate some of the ingredient's natural harshness, creating a delicate, balanced butter.

Add the garlic to a food processor with the butter, salt and parsley. Blitz until completely smooth and combined. You should expect the butter to take on a bright green colour from the parsley.

For the Dijon mayonnaise

Add the mayonnaise and mustard to a small mixing bowl and mix until even in colour.

For the burgers

Place a large, cast iron skillet on a very high heat. Slice open the brioche buns and toast them on the griddle for 1 minute.

Mould the ground beef into eight 150g balls. Gently flatten the beef balls onto the skillet to create burger patties. Cook evenly on both sides: less than 2 minutes per side for medium-rare, 2 minutes per side for medium, 3 minutes for medium-well and 4 minutes for well done. Season each burger with salt on both sides.

Once the burgers have cooked on both sides, place some caramelised onion on top of each one, before layering again with a slice of Swiss cheese.

At this point, we would normally cover the burgers with a metal cloche for a few seconds. A spray of water underneath generates steam, helping us ensure that the cheese is well melted and that the beef is perfectly cooked, yet pink and moist. Although optional, you could replicate this process at home with a wok cover or something similar.

Meanwhile, it's time to dress your buns! Spread the bottom half of each bun with garlic butter, and on the top halves spoon a good dollop of Dijon mayonnaise.

To serve

Once the cheese is melted, assemble the burgers by placing two on top of each other. Sandwich inside the burger buns and hold everything together with a wooden skewer.

Serve and eat immediately; we like to enjoy ours with some delicious rosemary salted fries.

Free State Kitchen
BOSTON CLAM CHOWDER

Having sampled some delicious chowders during our travels to the US we had to put one on our menu. The Boston clam chowder is a firm favourite with our regulars, particularly on a cold winter's day. You don't have to limit the chowder to just clams. You could add fish such as salmon, haddock or other shellfish like prawns.

Preparation time: 15 minutes | Cooking time: 40 minutes | Serves 4

Ingredients

1 large onion

4 sticks of celery

8 medium white potatoes (approximately 1 kilo), peeled and diced

200ml fish stock (we make a fresh fish stock in advance with fish bones, carrot, celery, bay leaves, onions and flat leaf parsely but you can use a pot of shop bought stock if a fresh stock is not available)

200g smoked streaky bacon, chopped

1 litre whole milk

150ml double cream

250g cooked frozen clams defrost for two hours before required (alternatively you could use fresh clams if they are available)

To serve:

2 tbsp of chopped fresh flat leaf parsley

Slices of fresh rye bread and butter (to serve)

Method

Finely dice the celery and onion and sweat in a pan with vegetable oil and butter for 10-15 minutes until well softened and beginning to colour. Add the diced potatoes and cover with whole milk, and bring to a gentle simmer being careful not to split the milk. This should take around 20 minutes.

Add fish stock and simmer until the potatoes are soft and beginning to collapse. In a frying pan, fry the finely chopped bacon until brown and crisp. Finish by blending half the soup, and adding double cream and parsley to the whole batch. Add in bacon pieces and adjust the seasoning if needed. At this point you can add the clams to the soup so they take on the residual heat of the soup. If you add the clams too soon they will become tough.

If you are using fresh clams you can cook them with the onion and celery. Once the onions and celery are softened add the washed clams into the pot with 150ml of water, cover the pan and shake occasionally. The clams should begin to open after 5 minutes of cooking. Remove the clams from the shells, pouring any broth in the shells into the chowder. Discard the shells that haven't opened. Cover the clams and set aside until the chowder broth is finished.

To serve

Pour the hot chowder into bowls, garnish with parsley and serve with rye bread and butter.

Street food with a social
CONSCIENCE

Social enterprise Fritto serves up real Italian food 'on the go', while tackling social issues through cooking workshops and mentoring activities.

Starting life at the Granby Four Streets Community Market in Toxteth, Fritto brings an authentic taste of Italy to mobile street food, catering, pop-up events and community markets around Liverpool, Manchester and Leeds.

Visiting a Fritto market stall or pop-up event means a feast of homemade Italian goodies, such as panzerotti – the famous Italian pasty made with soft pizza dough – and the delicious vegan donuts frittelle. You'll also fall in love with Fritto's arancini – which literally mean little oranges – deep fried, saffron-infused risotto balls with melting Italian cheese in the middle.

As part of its ethos, Fritto uses food as a tool to facilitate positive change in the lives of unemployed people, young offenders and other disadvantaged groups by offering volunteering opportunities and work experience, along with cookery workshops and mentoring.

"I believe in the joy and excitement that food can bring. With Fritto, I aim to improve people's confidence and self-esteem through cooking, sharing and eating together. Food is a universal language and has the power to make a real difference in people's lives, be it socially, in terms of skills and employment, or improving health and wellbeing," says Luca Sanvittore, the man behind Fritto.

"The majority of people who come along are used to eating ready meals. The aim of the workshops is to give them the basics of how to cook simple and affordable meals with healthy, fresh ingredients. We give them recipes they can take away and do at home."

Milan-born Luca came to Merseyside in 2010 to study a Masters degree in Criminology at the University of Liverpool. Five years later, he left his office job to follow his passion for cooking and do something more worthwhile.

Just months after launching his social enterprise, Luca's work has been recognised at the 2016 Liverpool Youth Awards for 'improving wellbeing and resilience of young people'.

So for a genuine taste of Italy, keep your eyes peeled for Fritto's next pop-up appearance and get involved with its workshops.

Fritto PANZEROTTI

The Italian pasty – a flavour-filled savoury turnover that looks like a mini calzone pizza. Originally hailing from southern and central Italy, they are now a globally popular snack.

Preparation time: 30 minutes plus rising the dough overnight | Cooking time: 3 minutes each | Makes 16

Ingredients

For the dough:

1kg strong white bread flour

1g fresh yeast

600ml water

20g salt

For the filling:

Passata

Grated mozzarella

Fresh basil

Oregano

Olive oil

Salt and pepper

Vegetable oil for frying

Method

For the dough

Dissolve the yeast in 500ml of water and separately dissolve the salt in the remaining 100ml.

Put the flour in a mixing bowl and make a large well in the centre. Pour in the water slowly, mix well and blend until all the flour has been incorporated. Add the water with salt and mix for a couple of minutes.

Transfer the dough onto a table and knead for at least 10 minutes until it becomes smooth and elastic.

Divide the dough into approximately 16 balls each weighing around 100g. Place the dough balls in a tray and cover with a lid or cling film and leave to rise over 24 hours at room temperature.

To make the panzerotti

Take a ball of dough, flatten and shape into a circle about 10cm in diameter.

Season the passata with salt, pepper, oregano and olive oil then spoon some of the sauce into the centre of the dough. Add a handful of mozzarella and a leaf of fresh basil, then fold in half and seal the edges, creating a 'calzone'.

Be sure to close the dough carefully so no filling escapes while frying. To seal your Panzerotti, use the flat side of a fork around the outer edge.

In a large pan, heat the oil to 190°c and carefully drop in your panzerotti. Cook on each side until golden brown, approximately 3 minutes.

Remove from the pan and dry any excess oil with kitchen roll. Enjoy straight away.

This recipe is great for experimenting with different fillings, such as spinach and ricotta or ham and cheese.

Just GORGE'US

Famed for its cakes and afternoon teas, Gorge'us is a vintage gem on the Wirral, where you'll find a great gluten-free range plus lots of savoury goodies.

"I'd always wanted to pick up the phone and say: 'Hello, Gorgeous'," says Ceri Newton, when she's asked how Gorge'us coffee shop got its name.

"And we do gorgeous things."

Gorge'us is justly famed for its superb selection of cakes that are baked fresh on the premises by Ceri and her fellow baker Kerry Tudor, around half of which are gluten-free. The shop has won local and national prizes for its cakes, including two Great Taste Awards for its Victoria sponge.

The mouth-watering selection includes such delights as coffee and walnut, chocolate, lemon drizzle, salted caramel, Turkish delight and orange and pistachio. Brownies, rocky road bars and shortbread can be found on the menu too.

The shop also makes bespoke wedding cakes – either 'naked' sponges for people to decorate themselves with fruit or flowers; or 'semi-naked' with a little buttercream so they can also be decorated at home; plus full fondant covered two and three-tier affairs.

For a shop that has such a reputation for its cakes, it's no surprise to find that Gorge'us has been consistently voted one of the best afternoon tea venues in Merseyside.

It's not just about the cakes though; there's a huge range of sandwiches, soups, jacket potatoes, salads, breakfasts, brunches and lunches on offer. Everything bar the bread is made fresh on the premises.

Inside, Gorge'us has a vintage vibe with bevelled mirrors, old fashioned china display cabinets and Cath Kidston wallpaper.

Ceri said: "We call it the parlour – it's like going into your nan's house and sitting down on a comfy sofa. There are standard lamps and table lamps. It's very, very vintage, which is my style."

Ceri started Gorge'us after an eclectic career that included managing sheltered housing, travelling the world working as a nanny, and then the turning point when she was grabbed during a bank robbery.

"This was something I'd always fancied doing, and the bank thing gives you a different outlook; you have to seize the day because you don't know what's going to happen," she said.

"I just have a love of baking and romantically thought how lovely it would be to be baking cakes and serving cakes. It's very enjoyable and very rewarding but it's hard work too, and I have a fabulous team to help me."

Gorge'us ORANGE AND PISTACHIO CAKE

A real tea time treat, combining the zing of citrus with the crunch of pistachios, all wrapped up in an indulgent frosting.

Preparation time: 10 minutes | Cooking time: 35 minutes | Serves 12

Ingredients

250g gluten-free self-raising flour blend

250g caster sugar

250g butter

4 large free-range eggs, beaten

1 tsp gluten-free baking powder

⅛ tsp xanthum gum

1 orange, zest

2 tbsp pistachio nuts plus extra for decorating

For the icing:

400g full fat cream cheese

100g icing sugar

1 tsp vanilla bean paste

½ medium orange, zest only

Strips of orange zest for decoration.

Method

Cream the butter and together sugar until pale, light and fluffy. Mix together the flour, baking powder and xanthum gum, and add to creamed mixture alternately with the beaten egg. Stir in the orange zest and nuts.

Divide between 2 x 23cm greased tins and bake at 180°c for 25 minutes or until golden and springy to touch. Cool.

To decorate

Beat together the cream cheese, icing sugar and vanilla until light and fluffy. Stir in the orange zest.

Use the icing to sandwich together the sponge layers and spread on top and around the sides.

Decorate with pistachio pieces and orange zest strips.

A twist on the
TRADITIONAL

Hardy's Kitchen aims to bring you something a little different. A twist on the traditional but always made with quality ingredients and a big pot of love.

Husband and wife team Lou and Matt Hardy opened Hardy's Kitchen in 2014 with a clear vision of what type of place they wanted it to be – a modern industrial setting serving traditional dishes with a bit of character. Taking something classic and adding something a little bit quirky is what they aim to do, whether that be switching up the way that it's cooked, seasoned or presented.

"We want to get the message across that there's so much out there that people can do with food, not to be put off by ingredients that are hard to get hold of or afraid to try things that are a little bit different," says Lou.

A resoundingly successful year went by which led them onto an exciting new venture, the 'Big Dub of Love' which is their 1979 VW camper van now used for street food projects and outside catering. From there it's gone from strength to strength and now they're doing festivals, events and weddings as well as private parties across the UK. Next year they're hoping to employ a second van, so they can travel out a bit further.

Each of their dishes uses quality ingredients – award-winning meats, fresh produce and local dairy and eggs. The vegetables they use are grown locally and their meat is supplied by Malamb Meats who are Red Tractor certified and have agreed to make sausages exclusively for them. Matt likes to dabble in all cuisines when conjuring up bold and punchy flavours, they like to keep it flexible in terms of what sort of food they serve as long as it still has their 'Hardy' twist on it. This means catering for all diets so you'll find lots of vegetarian and vegan dishes on their menu; the halloumi fries with sweet chilli dip are one of their bestsellers!

If the Hardys aren't in their café or camper van, they're probably busy looking after the food operation for other existing businesses. The goal is to design a menu that allows them to temporarily bring their kitchen staff and style of food into a new environment, this bridges the gap for the businesses that don't necessarily have the facilities or team to execute the food side of their business. The team recently collaborated with a pop-up Champagne bar in Liverpool and are embarking on more city centre collaborations before the end of 2016. It's no surprise that they were nominated for the Mersey Independent Business Awards this year!

Hardy's Kitchen & The Big Dub of Love

THE SPICY DUB SMASH BURGER WITH CAJUN HALLOUMI FRIES

Chef's tips: Cook your onions at the beginning so they are sitting to one side getting crispy. Sprinkle oregano onto one side of your burger before cooking to add awesome flavour, and don't over-salt, as it will cause it to shrink when cooking. The halloumi fries are at their very best when served hot and gooey, so make sure to cook these last.

Preparation time: 30-40 minutes | Cooking time: 10 minutes | Serves 1

Ingredients

Vegetable and olive oils
Salt and pepper
Plain flour, standard or gluten-free

For the burger:
6oz prime chuck steak, minced twice
½ tsp chilli flakes
½ tsp garlic powder/ground garlic
1½ tsp oregano
1 tsp cracked black pepper

For the harissa mayonnaise:
1 tsp harissa paste
1 dsp mayonnaise

For the homemade barbecue sauce:
3 dsp tomato ketchup
3 dsp brown sauce
1 dsp runny honey
1 tsp soy sauce
1 heaped tsp wholegrain mustard
1 tsp jalapeño, chopped

For the filling:
1 tsp paprika
1 tsp cayenne pepper
¼ large white onion, finely sliced
½ ripe avocado
½ lemon
1 knob of salted butter
50g chorizo, roughly cubed
50g Lancashire blue cheese (we love Blacksticks Blue!)

For the halloumi fries:
Halloumi, 1 block
Dried Cajun spice
Sweet chilli sauce
Sesame seeds
½ spring onion, finely chopped

To serve:
1 brioche bun, standard or gluten-free
1 handful of iceberg lettuce

Method

For the burger

Place the minced chuck steak into a bowl with the chilli flakes, garlic powder, oregano and cracked black pepper. Lightly massage the mince into a ball, making sure to incorporate the seasonings. Gently flatten the beef ball to create a burger patty shape.

To cook, drizzle olive oil onto a griddle pan and heat until softly sizzling. Place the burger into the pan and cook for 2½ minutes before turning. Allow the blood to rise to the top of the burger before flipping it back to the first side for a further minute of cooking. If you have a thermometer, a medium rare burger should be 70°c.

For the harissa mayonnaise

Add 1 tsp of harissa paste to a dessert spoon of mayonnaise. Season with sea salt and black pepper and stir to combine.

For the BBQ Sauce

Add the ketchup, brown sauce, honey, soy sauce, wholegrain mustard and jalapeños to a bowl and mix together.

For the filling

In a small bowl, mix 2 tbsp of your chosen flour with the paprika, cayenne pepper, salt and pepper. Add the chopped onions and mix until completely coated with the seasoned flour mix.

Fill a pan three inches deep with vegetable oil and place over a high heat. Test the temperature by carefully dropping in a piece of onion, if it sizzles and floats to the top of the pan, it's good to go! Add the rest of the onions, being careful to avoid any hot oil spitting from the pan, and fry until golden.

Remove with a slotted spoon and place on some paper towel to drain.

Meanwhile, take half an avocado and mash roughly in a bowl with the juice of half a lemon and some salt and pepper.

In a frying pan, heat the knob of butter with a drizzle of olive oil. Add the chorizo and cook for 40 seconds, while shaking the pan back and forth. Next add the Lancashire blue cheese, removing from the heat once completely melted.

For the halloumi fries

Slice the halloumi into cube or fry shapes and coat with gluten-free or plain flour and Cajun spice.

Heat some vegetable oil in a large saucepan to 180°c, or bubbling hot. Carefully drop the halloumi into the oil and cook until crispy and golden.

Drain on a paper towel and serve drizzled with sweet chilli sauce, sprinkled with sesame seeds and garnished with spring onions.

To serve

Lightly toast the brioche bun. Spoon a dollop of the harissa mayonnaise onto the bottom half before layering on pieces of iceberg lettuce. Top this with the avocado, followed by the beef patty, gooey melted cheese and chorizo, and finally the crispy onions. To finish, dollop some homemade BBQ sauce onto the lid of the brioche then carefully place it on top of the burger.

Kasbah Café Bazaar
MOROCCAN CHICKEN TAGINE WITH OLIVES AND CONFIT OF LEMON

Stepping into Kasbah is like travelling to Marrakesh without a passport. Sit back, relax, put your Fez hat on and enjoy the warmth of the Moroccan hospitality. Let Kasbah transport you to the hustle and bustle of the lively and colourful streets and souks of Marrakech with the unique smell, colourful lanterns, authentic Moroccan furniture and handcrafted decorations – all of which can be bought in the restaurant, even the music!

This dish came from Amine's grandmother Lala Ratiba, of whom he has fond memories with from spending time with her in the kitchen as a child: "This dish reflects my childhood back home. She was like an artist creating a masterpiece in her kitchen; I will always remember her secret box full of colourful spices including saffron, cumin, turmeric, ginger, paprika and cinnamon. Her food was always perfect and everything was made with such precision and love. She was a very quiet and wise lady, preparing food was the way she could express herself," says Amine. Here he shares this special recipe, so that you too can bring the taste of Morocco to your own kitchen.

Preparation time: 15 minutes | Cooking time: 45 minutes | Serves 2

Ingredients

1 tbsp clarified butter

2 tbsp olive oil

1 onion, roughly chopped

1 garlic clove, crushed

4 pieces of chicken, preferably on the bone for added flavour

½ confit of lemon

1 tsp ginger

1 tsp turmeric

Saffron, a pinch

1 tsp fresh parsley, chopped

1 tsp fresh coriander, chopped

1 tsp salt

1 tsp pepper

Water, a small glass

10 green olives

Method

For this recipe you will need a tagine pot, but if you can't get your hands on one a large pot, Dutch oven, slow cooker or casserole dish will do.

In the tagine, gently heat the butter and oil. Add the chopped onion and crushed garlic and cook for 5 minutes.

Next put in the chicken pieces. Add a quarter of the confit of lemon and all of the herbs and spices before gently stirring to combine.

Add a small glass of water to the sauce, and leave to simmer at a low heat for another 40 minutes.

You must check inside the pot at regular intervals; if the tagine is drying you will need to add more water.

Once cooked, decorate with the green olives and the remaining quarter of the confit of lemon.

Looking to the FUTURE

Created by Hugh Baird College in 2013, L20 Hotel School is tapping into some of the region's top culinary talent to educate and train the city's future superstar chefs.

The L20 Hotel School is not just a typical catering school. Founded in 2013, the school is part of Hugh Baird College situated on the outskirts of the city.

The aim of the school is to shape the future of the hospitality industry by providing education, training, work experience and inspiration for those taking their first steps into the industry.

The school is geared up just like a professional restaurant and in fact they also run their own L20 Restaurant – The L20 Hotel School has a team of dedicated teaching staff, a head chef, a sous chef, a commercial coordinator, a restaurant supervisor and a small team of apprentices, who with students, run the core of the business.

As a team they provide hot and cold food and drink all day through the various eateries and bars as well as servicing functions and providing hospitality for conferences, meetings and events.

In order to ensure they maintain standards and remain at the cutting edge of the industry, they also have regular visits from leaders of the UK hospitality industry to work alongside students and staff. These include the likes of Michelin-starred chefs Nigel Haworth, Kenny Atkinson and Mark Greenaway, Channel 4's Sunday Brunch chef/presenter Simon Rimmer

as well as highly-regarded local chefs such as Matt Worswick and Steven Burgess.

The L20 Hotel School is all about student success, raising standards, nurturing talent and instilling in the students the attitude needed to be successful in the hospitality world. Everything the Hotel School do is geared towards creating opportunities that lead onto full-time employment in the industry. And on that front they have succeeded, with a large number of past learners now working in leading UK restaurants thanks to links forged in the kitchens of the L20 Hotel School.

The L20 Restaurant is also a popular dining destination with outstanding TripAdvisor reviews and many diners returning week after week.

The feel is contemporary yet inviting and there's front of house service to match. It boasts a lounge for pre-dinner drinks, canapé receptions or an informal meeting while the dining area can accommodate up to 50 guests, or for functions and banquets, 90 guests can be seated with ease.

So if you want to test the culinary skills of the city's future chef stars, be sure to head down and uncover Liverpool's best kept dining secret.

L20 Hotel School

BOOTLE

L20 RESTAURANT
www.L20restaurant.co.uk
0151 353 4518

L20
RESTAURANT

DUCK BREAST, CROQUETTES, DAUPHINOISE POTATOES AND STAR ANISE JUS

A multi-layered dish where many of the parts need to be prepared a day in advance.
Served with a creamy broccoli purée, it's a real dinner party show-stopper.

Preparation time: 1 day | Cooking time: 5-6 hours | Serves 10

Ingredients

2 whole Goosnargh ducks

For the duck breast brine:

8 prepped duck breast pieces

150g salt

4 juniper berries, 6 coriander seeds and 3 bay leaves

2 litres water

For the duck confit:

8 duck legs

20g salt and 15g thyme

1 orange

2 garlic cloves, crushed and 2 shallots, finely diced

3 litre vegetable oil

100ml duck star anise sauce (see method)

2 whole eggs beaten

200g plain flour and 300g panko breadcrumbs

For the sauce:

Duck carcasses

2 sticks of celery, ½ onion, 2 carrots, 1 leek, 2 shallots, 1 garlic clove and 2 sprigs thyme

1 litre red wine, 2 tbsp red currant jelly and 4 star anise

For the dauphinoise potatoes:

10 Desiree potatoes

3 garlic cloves, crushed and 3 sprigs thyme

500ml double cream and 250g butter

Method

For the duck

Remove the giblets from inside. Remove the legs and breast, but retain the carcasses.

Trim any excess fat and skin from the breasts. Halve the duck breasts lengthways and score the fat. Retain skin trimmings.

For the duck breast brine

Combine all of the ingredients, except the duck breasts, in a large pan and bring to the boil until the salt dissolves. Cool for 2 hours, then submerge the duck breast in the brine. Refrigerate for 24 hours.

For the duck confit

Place the duck legs in a tray skin side up. Sprinkle with salt and leave for 24 hours. Rinse the legs and pat dry. Put the duck legs, oil, thyme and garlic in a deep tray with the juice and the skin of the orange. Cover the tray tightly in tinfoil.

Cook at 130°c for 3 hours until the meat is tender. Allow to cool and then pick the meat off the bone discarding the bones and skin. Sauté the shallots over a medium heat until soft. When cool combine the meat and duck sauce.

Roll the mixture into balls approximately 30 grams in weight. Refrigerate for 30 minutes.

Roll each ball in the flour, beaten egg and breadcrumbs.

For the sauce

Roast the duck carcasses with the onion, celery, leeks and carrots at 190°c for 25 minutes until the carcasses are golden brown. Transfer to a pan and cover with cold water. Boil then simmer for 4 hours. Strain and cool overnight. Remove the top layer of fat from the stock.

Fry the shallots with the garlic, thyme and star anise for 3 minutes. Add red wine and reduce in volume by half. Add the duck stock and reduce by a third. Add the redcurrant jelly and pass through a fine strainer. Season to taste.

For the dauphinoise potatoes

Peel and thinly slice the potatoes. Bring the cream, butter, garlic, thyme to boil then allow to cool and infuse. Strain. Line a large baking tray with greaseproof paper. Layer the sliced potatoes in the tray and pour over the infused cream. Bake at 170°c for 25 minutes.

When cool, cover the top of the potatoes with greaseproof paper and press down with another tray. Refrigerate overnight then divide into 8 portions.

To serve

Heat the potatoes for 15 minutes at to 175°c. Fry the duck breasts for approximately four minutes each side. Deep fry the croquettes at 175°c for 6 minutes until golden brown. Warm the duck sauce through in a saucepan.

Know your CHEESE

From cheese cakes, hampers and monthly Cheese School classes, The Liverpool Cheese Company is the city's first specialist shop to share an appreciation of the very best in British, Irish and European cheeses on Merseyside.

"Cheese is a magical product, and many people are passionate about it. It is, however, rural rather than urban. There aren't any cows in Liverpool," points out Vickie Anderson, who owns the Liverpool Cheese Company.

"So we don't make our own cheese. But we do mature and look after the cheeses we source from the various farms and dairies."

Marking 10 years in business in 2016, Vickie took the plunge to open the city's first specialist cheese shop because there was nowhere for her to buy decent cheese and she soon discovered that many other people shared her passion.

Her vision was to persuade people to shop and eat in a different way and learn about what they're buying when she opened the business in a Grade II listed former dairy in Woolton Village.

"Getting people to understand the provenance of what they eat and the benefits of independent shopping is something which has grown greatly in the past 10 years," said Vickie.

"People queue for over an hour outside the shop at Christmas – pictures of the cheese queue abound on social media – but we still spend time letting people taste and choose their cheese. They ask us what's good at the moment and we tell them how to keep it and serve it, along with a little quirky history of the cheese and its maker. People like the personal service."

The Liverpool Cheese Company stocks more than 200 varieties at any one time. Around 70 per cent are British and Irish cheeses, with European cheeses making up the full complement. Vickie's own favourites include Gorwydd Caerphilly.

"It is a beautifully made, unpasteurised cheese" she says. "We like the sort of cheese which is made by cows known by name to the cheesemaker."

The award winning cheese wedding cakes are signatures of The Liverpool Cheese Company, along with Cheese School, which is run twice a month in the upstairs room at the Clove Hitch on Hope Street. A dozen cheeses are paired with wines, gins, whiskies or ciders, and there is the opportunity to test and learn about the different taste combinations.

Vickie's enthusiasm for good cheese stretches across the city because The Liverpool Cheese Company is a regular at farmers markets and also supplies a number of pubs, cafés and restaurants.

Vickie said: "If you've spent some time in Liverpool, the chances are you've eaten a piece of our cheese."

Liverpool Cheese Company
BALTIC FONDUE

A super simple but very effective cheese recipe, incorporating two different types of cheese plus alcohol in an indulgent fondue that's perfect for sharing with friends.

Preparation time: 5 minutes | Cooking time: 10 minutes | Serves 4-6

Ingredients

1 large garlic clove, halved

2 tsp cornflour

3 tbsp kirsch

150ml medium dry white wine, or try a good local beer instead

1tsp lemon juice

350g Baltic cheese

100g Fontina cheese

Walnut bread and crudites to serve

Method

Rub the garlic around the base of a fondue pot or heavy based saucepan.

Blend the cornflour and kirsch together to form a smooth paste. Put the wine or beer, lemon juice, cheese and cornflour mixture into the pot and bring to the boil over a low heat stirring continuously.

Simmer for a few minutes.

To serve

Serve the fondue with walnut bread and crudites to dip in, and enjoy.

Another LEVEL

When the UK's largest independent drinks manufacturer and distributor bought Liverpool Gin in May 2016, some were concerned what they had in store for the popular local brand. But they needn't have worried. With very real connections to the city of their own, Halewood have already shown they will grow the brand without losing sight of what made it work so well in the first place.

Originally founded by Liverpool Organic Brewery owner Mark Hensby and Belvedere pub licensee John O'Dowd in 2012, Liverpool Gin has been a real local success story.

Liverpool's docks have long welcomed many of the botanicals and grain spirit that combine to create gin, and with their distillery based just a stone's throw from the city's original Bank Hall distillery, Liverpool Gin quickly established a strong local following and a large range of stockists across the north-west.

After four years of growth, an approach was made to Halewood International, the Huyton drinks firm behind Lambrini and Crabbie's ginger beer, about buying the brand. For them, it was a no-brainer.

"We knew straight away it was a good fit for us," said Angel Gregory, Head of Spirits & Trade Marketing at Halewood.

"It was a strong Liverpool brand with a distillery in the city and being Merseyside-based ourselves with a successful gin brand in its own right, Whitley Neill Gin, we knew we could take Liverpool Gin forward. "

Within just a matter of months Halewood had already started expanding by launching an organic potato-based vodka (Liverpool Vodka) while the gin is now stocked in Selfridges and Harvey Nichols as well as specialist outlets such as Mr Fogg's Gin Parlour in Covent Garden.

With such an explosion of gin producers in the UK, Angel says the audience has grown and developed dramatically in recent years.

"Traditionally gin was seen as an older person's drink," she said. "But these days it's increasingly popular with those 25 and up. The split used to be 60/40 women to men but is now 50/50 and these 'new' drinkers are much more likely to explore fresh tastes and styles, so there really is something for everyone out there."

So with us so spoilt for choice when it comes to 'mother's ruin', what is Angel's personal favourite gin tipple?

"I'd probably go for a simple gin with bitter lemon," she says. "Or if I really fancy something a bit different then there's a Negroni (gin, Campari, vermouth) or Martinez; gin, rosso vermouth, Maraschino and a twist of orange. Delicious."

Liverpool: since 1207

LIVERPOOL GIN

SMALL BATCH ENGLISH GIN

43%Vol Product of England 70cl℮

Liverpool Gin
GIN AND TONIC

Everyone has their own opinion of which tonic and garnish goes best with their favourite gin. We recommend Fever Tree with a wedge of watermelon for a refreshing, full-flavoured finish.

Preparation time: 5 minutes | Serves 1

Ingredients

35ml Liverpool Gin

1 bottle of Fever Tree tonic water

1 wedge of watermelon

Method

Add 35ml Liverpool Gin to a balloon glass.

Top with a premium tonic water – we prefer Fever Tree but you may have your own favourite.

Garnish with a wedge of watermelon and serve with plenty of ice.

Liverpool Gin
CLOVER CLUB

The Clover Club pre-dates Prohibition, and is named for the Philadelphia men's club of the same name.

Preparation time: 5 minutes | Serves 1

Ingredients

50ml Liverpool Gin

Dash lemon juice

Dash raspberry syrup

Method

Add 50ml Liverpool Gin to a shaker filled with ice.

Add a dash of lemon juice and a dash of raspberry syrup. Shake and strain into a cocktail glass.

Garnish with a speared raspberry to serve.

Special BREW

Since their launch in 2008, Liverpool Organic Brewery has gone from strength to strength, now supplying pubs, bars and restaurants across the UK with their unique brews.

Liverpool Organic Brewery exists for just one purpose; to create great-tasting, handcrafted beers using only the finest ingredients. And thanks to the toil of managing director Mark Hensby and his team, it's something that they have achieved, year-in, year-out since they launched in 2008.

An independent craft brewery based in Kirkdale in Liverpool, they spent their first year of trading honing their skills and recipes until they were happy to make their public debut. Since then, they've never looked back and their customer base continues to grow to this day.

In fact, their list of stockists reads like a who's who of the pubs, bars, cafés and restaurants of the northwest, with over 100 venues selling their brews and that's not including the countless beer shops, off licences, delis and other shops they also supply.

"We've probably reached – and hopefully pleased – every real ale lover in the north west," says Mark. "But we like to think we've also converted quite a few palates along the way too.

"Top quality beer shouldn't be about mass production, discount offers or huge marketing budgets but nor should it be the preserve of a select few," he added. "That's why we're so proud of our broad range of cask and bottled lagers, pale ales, bitters and stouts, as it offers something for every taste and experience."

And he's right, the range of ales on offer is certainly impressive; there are the core beers such as their Best Bitter (ABV 4.2%) with its hoppy bitterness balanced with pale malts and a hint of citrus fruit or their Liverpool Pale Ale (ABV 4%) which has dry hoppy notes with floral complexity giving way to spicy tones and a slightly creamy malt finish. Other popular beers include the Styrian Pale Ale (ABV 4.2%) and the somewhat stronger Shipwreck IPA (ABV 6.2%) with grapefruit, aniseed and peach notes featuring in its hoppy bite.

And it's not just the north-west that has succumbed to their organic charms. Very much at the forefront of the microbrewery and craft ale boom in the UK, they've also secured regular customers from as far afield as London, Leeds, Bristol, Newcastle and Glasgow.

So what makes them stand out? Over to Mark again…

"All micro breweries claim to use the best ingredients but if they are not organic they are not the best. We are one of only a handful of organic breweries out of 1500 in the UK – so we are confident our product stands out."

So what exactly is organic beer? And why should real ale fans yet to be converted give it a go?

Organic beer has a lack of carcinogenic pesticides on the ingredients. Its production also promotes biodiversity, helps wildlife, and provides a mixed and sustainable ecology for flora and fauna to thrive. It means it's more expensive to produce but generally those costs are absorbed by the brewery and beer prices are very competitive.

But for Liverpool Organic Brewery, the job doesn't start and finish with brewing and supplying real ale. They are also heavily involved in a range of events and beer festivals – including some of their own – such as The St George's Hall Beer Fest which features over 200 beers and ciders from across the UK and has become a staple part of the Liverpool events calendar. These events are not just confined to Liverpool either; they are part of the Blackpool Beer and Cider Festival held in the spring and the Southport Beer and Folk Festival held each summer, an event which in 2016 showcased their 1000th brew. To mark the occasion the team created a new punchy, hoppy IPA appropriately titled 'Grand'.

Keen to promote interest in organic beer and its production process, they also run brewery tours so fans of the company can meet the team and learn about the brewing process from start to finish, as well as discuss malt and hop varieties and experience a taste of the working day at the brewery.

With interest in organic brewing growing all the time, it all adds up to a successful formula which is why Liverpool Organic Brewery expect the next eight years to be even more successful than the last.

A Fistful of FLAVOUR

Taking inspiration from the restaurants and streets of Guadalajara – Lucha Libre brings inventive and exciting food cooked with lots of love and full of flavour.

Inspired by a couple of trips to Mexico several years ago, Alex Hannah decided to set up the concept of Lucha Libre to reflect his experiences there. Along with his brother Christian and their longtime partners in crime Dave Roche and Conor Foley, together they embarked on a journey that is still going strong 5 years later.

Situated in the heart of Liverpool on Wood Street, Lucha Libre has grown from strength to strength serving modern twists on street food classics from Guadalajara such as quesadillas, tamales, tostadas and of course the famous tacos. Lucha Libre is about modern Mexican eating as opposed to the more commonly found 'Tex-Mex' style.

"Having spent a lot of time in Mexico we wanted to reflect what is really happening in downtown Guadalajara rather than the stereotypical image of sombreros, donkeys and greasy deep fried tex-mex food," says Alex. The food at Lucha Libre is very progressive. Whilst they have a lot of classic style dishes on the menu, they constantly strive to keep the offering exciting and fresh by changing the menu seasonally and by also offering specials across the year. Innovation is key in everything they do.

They only use the finest imported Mexican ingredients and combine it with the very best locally sourced meat, fruit and veg. The meat is generally slow-cooked or marinated for many hours and they have a huge focus on vegetarian cuisine which is very apparent in Mexican culture. Lucha are well known for their famous soft shell tacos which are filled with the vibrant colours and inviting smells of the contents, they almost look too good to eat – almost.

Now their cocktail menu is a thing of beauty, it has intricate illustrations of their range of beverages which is a huge part of what they do. Hangovers are a thing of the past here because they only use the very best tequilas and mezcals – it has to be 100% agave or it isn't 100% Mexican!

Lucha Libre aspires to provide somewhere that feels as comfortable for lunch and dinner as it does for cocktails, dancing and partying in the evening. A social hub where people from all walks of life are welcome and feel appreciated.

Lucha Libre
CAULIFLOWER AND BEETROOT TACO

What started as a daily special quickly found it's way onto our menu due to high demand and passionate loyal Lucha veggies.

Preparation time: 15 minutes | Cooking time: 35 minutes | Serves 4

Ingredients

For the turmeric batter:

330ml Mexican lager

200g plain flour

1 tsp baking powder

½ tsp turmeric

45ml malt vinegar

For the beetroot purée:

Cooked beetroot, 1 pack

1 clove of garlic, thinly sliced

2 stalks fresh rosemary

Salt and pepper

250ml vegetable oil

For the battered cauliflower:

1 half head of cauliflower, florets separated evenly

Plain flour for dusting

To serve:

12 small soft corn tortillas

To garnish:

Parmesan shavings

Pomegranate seeds

Pea shoots

Method

For the turmeric batter

In a mixing bowl, whisk the ingredients together until smooth. If it's too lumpy you can pass it through a colander. Leave it to rest while preparing the other ingredients so that the yeast has a chance to activate.

For the beetroot purée

Place all of the ingredients except the vegetable oil onto a baking tray and cover with tin foil. Bake in the oven at 180° degrees for 25 minutes.

Once cooked remove the foil and take out the rosemary stalks, then place the remaining cooked ingredients into a food processor and blitz. While blending, gradually add the vegetable oil until the mixture is a smooth consistency.

For the battered cauliflower

Parboil the cauliflower florets for 1 minute, then drain thoroughly and place immediately into ice-cold water to cool.

Pat the cauliflower dry with some kitchen towel before lightly coating each floret in plain flour.

Next dip the florets into the beer-batter mix until evenly covered, before gently dropping them into a pan of piping hot vegetable oil.

Fry for 3-4 minutes, or until the batter turns golden brown in colour.

Remove the florets from the oil using a slotted spoon and place them on kitchen towel to drain.

To serve

Heat the tacos in a dry, non-stick pan for 1 minute. To retain their moisture, sprinkle a little water on each.

Next coat each taco with some beetroot purée, layer with a couple of cauliflower florets and garnish with Parmesan shavings, pomegranate seeds and pea shoots.

Passion on a PLATE

A proudly independent and multi-award winning deli, restaurant and bar in Liverpool recreating the wonderful Catalan and Spanish dining culture.

Lunya is Peter and Elaine Kinsella's homage to Catalunya and Spain. They are incredibly passionate about the Spanish food and drink scene as well as the whole culture of eating out in the glorious country. Both the food served in the restaurant and the produce available in the deli has made it a place where all foodies can eat, drink and socialise comfortably as if they were in their own home.

This is the dream job for Peter and Elaine who both left their respective careers and sold everything to pursue their love for food. "We have created something partly to give us the very best environment to work in and also to share our passion for food – we are still learning everyday but we are very proud owners of what we think is a truly unique place," says Elaine.

Catalan inspired artwork is displayed all around the walls of the restaurant, as well as unusual papier mâché statues imported from Barcelona. They are made to centuries old papier mâché techniques and decorated in a Gaudi-esque style with a kaleidoscope and mosaic of colours.

For Lunya, providing top quality products is their guiding force to everything they do day-to-day. Fish, meat and vegetables are fresh from source using local butchers, fishmongers and farmers who are the cream of the crop in the UK, including Edge Butchers and Ward's Fish. They also source only the finest of artisan Catalan and Spanish ingredients in order to bring us the most authentic deli around – it is due to this fusion of local and Spanish produce that Lunya gets its truly distinct flavour. The duo have close relationships with their Spanish producers and suppliers. Peter likes to visit different regions to meet farmers, cheese makers, fishermen and ham curers conducive to finding goods that are worthy of its place in the deli. They can proudly boast that they have met most of the people who grow or make the food they have in the deli.

The deli is a temple of flavours and textures of Catalunya with bits of local and international produce that complement the Spanish produce. "It's a delightful range of sights, aromas and things to pick up and look at, we are always on the look out for more things we can add to the deli that would fit the bill," says Peter. They stock everything from cheeses (with what is believed to be the world's largest selection of Spanish cheese outside of Spain, with more than 40 artisan cheeses from across Spain) and homemade sourdough bread to spirits and bottles of the most lavish wines. Not forgetting their superb collection of jamón which is hand-carved fresh from the bone. If you don't live in Liverpool then don't fret because everything they sell in the deli can be bought on their website which is the largest Spanish online food and drink store in the UK.

'Passion on a plate' is their motto for the food served at Lunya, they have one of the most extensive menus in the country probably due to the myriad of ingredients they have available. Dishes change with the seasona and with the ideas and inspirations of their chefs and they also cater for most dietary requirements including vegetarians, vegans and gluten-free diets. There is something for all kinds of people at all times of the day at Lunya, from breakfast right through to supper.

Many of the dishes honour the heritage and culture of Catalunya for example the Catalan migas – a traditional Spanish breakfast using chorizo, morcilla and pancetta or try the perfect blend of Liverpool and Catalunya, the Catalan Scouse. For a special occasion, you can order the most spectacular roast suckling pig imported from Segovia and served in true Spanish style with the whole pig at the table. Paella is made fresh to order and of course the tapas menu is something to be admired, whether it's meat, fish, veg, hot, cold, grilled or fried – you can be sure that is going to be delicious and bursting with flavour.

Each month they host wonderful food and drink events, including their legendary gourmet food and wine nights which feature the very best of Catalan and Spanish cuisine paired with the perfect unique wines. They also hold gin, wine and cheese tastings and you can even attend a masterclass to learn the art of ham carving.

The Guardian, Times, Sunday Times, Independent and Daily Telegraph have all included Lunya in their lists of top restaurants in the UK and they have won numerous awards over the past few years. They featured in the Good Food Guide winning the title of North West Restaurant of the Year for an unprecedented two years running and the fact that they have tens of thousands of repeat customers is testament to how successful they are – so successful in fact that they opened a second Lunya in Manchester in late 2015.

Lunya

Life's too short to drink cheap wine!

Lunya
GARBANZOS WITH BUTTERNUT SQUASH & APRICOT

The origins of this dish grew from a trip Peter took to Navarra in 2006 and further developed by our head chefs. Near the chickpea fields between Navarra and Zamora, he found a roadside restaurant where he was served a simple meal of garbanzos. He still claims this to be one of the best dishes he has ever tasted. Typically garbanzos are served with cumin and spinach, yet our dish retains this moorish flavour with the addition of butternut squash and apricots. These add fabulous texture and a hint of sweetness.

Preparation time: 30 minutes plus 1 night soaking | Cooking time: 90 minutes | Serves 4-8

Ingredients

1kg dried chickpeas, soaked in cold water overnight then drained (you could use 1kg of canned chickpeas)

½ tsp bicarbonate of soda

1 large butternut squash, cut into 1cm cubes

2 carrots, cut into 1cm cubes

40ml olive oil

1 medium sized onion, finely chopped

2 dried guindilla chillies, finely chopped (can substitute with dried peppers)

4 garlic cloves, crushed

1 dsp cumin

1 tsp toasted cumin seeds

1 dsp cinnamon

½ tsp turmeric

Saffron, 20 strands

2 tsp ras el hanout

2 dsp tomato purée

200ml sofrito (can alternatively replace this with passata and by doubling the quantity of onion stated in the recipe)

200g dried apricots, soaked in water for 2 hours then diced

Salt and pepper to taste

1 packet fresh coriander, roughly chopped

Seeds of half a pomegranate

50g sliced almonds, lightly toasted

50ml pomegranate molasses

Method

Place the chickpeas in a pan of fresh water and bring to the boil. Cook for 90-120 minutes or until soft. Remove from the heat and add the bicarbonate of soda. Do not drain!

Toss the butternut squash and carrots in olive oil and place into a roasting tin. Roast in the oven at 170°c for 15 minutes.

Tip the chopped onions, guindilla chillies, garlic, herbs and spices into a frying pan with some olive oil and cook over a medium heat for 10 minutes.

Add the tomato purée and fry for a further 5 minutes. Reduce to a low heat, pour in the sofrito and cook for another 5 minutes. Add some water if it gets too dry.

Transfer the contents of the frying pan into the pan with the chickpeas. Add the roasted vegetables and apricots and stir well.

Bring to a very slow simmer, test for seasoning and add salt and pepper to taste. Leave to simmer on a low heat for about 1 hour. By this point the sauce will have thickened and will be coating the chickpeas. You cannot over cook this. If it gets too dry, just add a little water. Add the coriander 10 minutes prior to serving.

To serve

Portion into large bowls, sprinkle over the pomegranate seeds, toasted, sliced almonds and drizzle with pomegranate molasses.

Keeping it in
THE FAMILY

With a famous Scouse recipe passed down through three generations of their family, Maggie Mays' story is built on foundations of hearty cooking and the strong bonds of a close family.

When John Lea used to watch his mother making her Scouse recipe as a child, little did he know it would form the backbone of a family business that has thrived for over 20 years.

Maggie Mays began life in 1996 when John's wife Susan decided to open her own café after running food concessions in a range of Liverpool pubs. John, who had been in the Merchant Navy, was recruited chef, while his daughter Carly, and three years later his son, Andy, also joined the fold.

They quickly became famous for their Scouse recipe, which they still make today, in exactly the way John's mum taught him.

Originally brought to these shores by Scandinavian seamen in the 18th century, Scouse is essentially a meat stew, usually made with lamb or beef and a mix of vegetables. It became a staple of the Liverpudlian diet and eventually became the dish that gave them their nickname.

So what makes the Maggie Mays Scouse so special?

"We cook the meat slowly to get that beautiful texture and bring out its full flavour," John says. "When we first started making it, Scouse wasn't that readily available but its definitely started making a comeback recently."

John and Susan still work every day alongside their children and the family have always tried to reach out to the community during their time in business. They were instrumental in bringing a street paving art competition to Bold Street, which brought together artists from as far afield as Mexico, California, Spain and Holland, while they have always had a charitable arm and have recently begun a relationship with St Vincents School, a specialist school for sensory impairment.

But it's the heart-warming, home-cooked food that's the real story here. Favourites include their Pea Wack soup (a pea and vegetable soup with lentils and pearl barley) as well as their Wet Nellies (a kind of Liverpudlian take on bread pudding). Meanwhile, their Scouse recipe is so popular that for a time they sold it in pouches across the supermarkets of the north-west. An issue with their manufacturer has halted that temporarily but with a new company now on board, they expect to be back on sale in 2017.

And while the future plans look exciting – alongside the Scouse pouch relaunch they are soon to start opening during the evenings at weekends – one thing is for sure at Maggie Mays, the family will always stay at the centre of this heart-warming local business.

Maggie Mays
CAFE
BAR
Tel · 709 · 7600

Maggie May's
SCOUSE

This recipe has been passed down by Annie Lea, mother of owner John and grandmother of Carly and Andy, and is still made exactly the same way today. The beef is sourced from Clarke's The Butchers, a family butchers on Allerton Road, but if you can't make it there, just make sure you buy local if you can.

Preparation time: 30 minutes | Cooking time: 2.5 hours | Serves 4

Ingredients

1 knob lard or beef dripping

700g diced chuck steak, preferably Welsh black beef

2 bay leaves

1 sprig thyme

400g diced onion, cut into 1cm pieces

350g diced swede, cut into 1.5cm cubes

350g carrots, cut into 1.5cm cubes

600g peeled and diced potatoes (ideally Maris Piper), cut into 1.5 cm cubes

2 litres beef stock

Salt and pepper for seasoning

Method

First of all, try to use organically sourced produce if you can. This without doubt adds flavour and makes all the difference to your Scouse. With the potatoes, we recommend Maris Piper. These are versatile and flavoursome and readily available from all good stockists.

Heat a knob of lard or beef dripping in a large saucepan over a medium heat (180°c) for about a minute.

Add the diced chuck steak and stir occasionally to prevent sticking. Cook carefully until the meat is evenly browned on all sides. Season with salt and pepper.

Add the onions and cook until they are soft.

Add 500ml of your beef stock and boil until the liquid has reduced by half.

Add the diced and peeled carrot, swede and half of the potato, followed by bay leaves and the sprig of thyme.

Then add in the rest of the beef stock, bring to the boil and simmer for 30 minutes.

Add in the rest of the potato and simmer for 90 minutes until the meat is tender. Check the seasoning and serve.

We prefer to split the potatoes as the first portion will add flavour and thicken the sauce while the last portion will give the traditional rustic look of a typical bowl of Scouse.

To serve

Maggie May's original Scouse is served in the traditional way – with pickled beetroot and pickled cabbage, chunky sliced white bread and butter. We also love a little HP Sauce in ours but that's up to you.

Food for LIFE

Matta's are all about broadening people's horizons on different cultures as well as educating them on leading a healthier lifestyle.

It's been more than three decades since Matta's relocated to Bold Street from Granby. They've become much more than a grocery store since then and are now considered an imperative asset to Liverpool. The family business is owned by Dalip Matta and his siblings Deepak and Anjana who have worked hard to plant Matta's firmly on the culinary map.

Matta's specialise in international food but have recently veered more towards the health food range, especially now more and more people are becoming health conscientious. The store is an Aladdin's cave of superfoods, organic vegetables, rare spices and foreign delicacies – a melting pot of different classes and cultures, there truly is something for everyone.

If you come into the store regularly, you're bound to bump into someone you know. There is a real community of food lovers there, "You have the Chinese buying Indian spices, the Mexican buying Thai products, that's what we love about this place, integration," says Dalip. With him being a health coach, he often offers health advice for the customers who need help with purchasing products; it's not just about selling products

for Dalip, it's about helping the community. "We regularly get told that we're a throwback to a bygone era when retail was much more of a personal experience when food shopping."

Liverpool's increasing diversity has enabled them to expand their range of fresh produce and in-house packaged health foods tenfold over the last five years. Regular food tastings are held in-store, allowing customers to sample different sauces and chutneys and local foragers and farmers often bring in goods such as samphire, strawberries, kale and asparagus when in season. Not to mention the secret Matta's curry blend which is notoriously well-known across the globe – it's an old family recipe which can't be found anywhere else in the world.

Looking forward, Matta's hope to expand by opening an eco-friendly café with a rooftop garden where they would serve a variety of healthy dishes. Dalip would also like to open a well-being centre where he can host yoga and meditation classes – both projects encapsulate the Matta's ethos of healthy living. It's clear that Matta's are here for the long haul – here is to many more decades to come.

Matta's LENTIL CURRY

What makes this recipe unique is the special-blend curry powder, which was made into to a family recipe dating back more than 40 years is only available in Matta's. My sister loves to experiment with food and blends both north and south Indian flavours for this dish. We also like to incorporate some less conventional ingredients, such as the bottle gourd. Otherwise known as a dudhi or lauki this vegetable has many health benefits, but is only found in Asian food shops. This dish is best accompanied with basmati rice, cooked with some panch puran (Indian five spice); and you will also need a good, large pan or pressure cooker.

Preparation time: 20-30 minutes | Cooking time: 1 hour 15 minutes | Serves 6-8

Ingredients

1 large aubergine

1 butternut squash or bottle gourd

500g Heera toor dhal

3 large onions

Oil for frying, you could use ground nut, sunflower or coconut

Fresh stem ginger, a two-inch piece

Fresh garlic, 5 cloves

3 fresh green chillies

1 tsp Heera black cumin seeds

2 tsp Rajah black mustard seeds

Curry leaves, 20 fresh or 25 dried

Chopped tomatoes, 1 can (we recommend organic)

2 fresh tomatoes

1-2 tbsp tomato purée

2 heaped tsp Rajah coriander powder

1 tsp Rajah ground cumin

1 tsp Rajah turmeric

1 tsp Rajah garam masala

½ tsp Rajah chilli powder (optional)

2-3 tsp special-blend curry powder

2 tsp Himalayan pink salt

Fresh coriander, 1 bunch

4-5 baby aubergines, (optional)

For the riata:

A vegan soya lemon desert (125g each), or the equivalent quantity of natural or Greek style yoghurt

1 fresh tomato

Fresh coriander, a sprinkling

Fresh chilli, to garnish

Method

First of all, fill a large pan with water and bring it to the boil.

Dice the large aubergine and the butternut squash into one-inch squares. Then chop all of the remaining fresh ingredients, except the curry leaves, so that you can relax and enjoy the cooking experience (and avoid burning your onions!).

Wash the toor dhal until the water runs clear and free from starch.

When the water is bubbling, gently tip in the toor dhal, the aubergine and butternut squash. Leave on a moderate heat for 40 minutes. After a while you will notice that some starch begins to settle on the surface of the water. At regular intervals, remove this with a ladle.

Meanwhile, start frying the onions in some oil. I like to take my time, using only a moderate heat and allowing the onions to become transparent. Next add the ginger, garlic and chillies to the pan and fry until slightly golden in colour. Then pour in the black cumin seeds, black mustard seeds and curry leaves. Continue to fry for a further minute before adding the tinned tomatoes, fresh tomatoes and tomato purée. Cook for 3-4 minutes more and then put in the coriander powder, ground cumin, turmeric, garam masala, optional chilli powder, special-blend curry powder and the Himalayan pink salt. Continue to fry on a low heat for 3-4 minutes, by which point you will notice that some of the oil and spices have cooked off.

Check the consistency of the lentils and, if cooked to your liking, pour in the mixture of onions and spices (the tarka). Cook on a high heat for 3-5 minutes, then reduce to a very low heat and add the chopped coriander. Cook for about 5 minutes.

In the meantime, slice the baby aubergines in half and cook them on a griddle. Put to one side to use for garnishing.

For the riata

You will need a vegan soya lemon dessert, some fresh tomato and coriander. Mix to combine and sprinkle with fresh chilli for a bit of a kick. This can easily be made with natural or Greek style yoghurt. The options are endless: it's up to the cook!

To serve

Garnish with the baby aubergine, and serve alongside Indian five spice flavoured basmati rice and the riata, and accompanied by your family and friends.

Matta's
RAW RICE PAPER ROLLS

I chose to share this dish because of its connection to my own personal journey with food. Not only does it adhere to a healthy lifestyle, but it also celebrates the array of quality ingredients Matta's International Foods' has to offer. Inspired by various evolving cuisines with a world taste, this dish is gluten-free and vegan. You can use any vegetables you like, but we recommend organic.

Preparation time: 30-40 minutes, 20-30 minutes to assemble | Serves 10 as a starter, or 4 for a main course.

Ingredients

250g goji berries

250g cashew nuts

200ml orange juice, we use organic

1 avocado

1 sweet mango

1 small raw green Thai papaya

10ml orange blossom water

1 large handful of beansprouts

10ml tamari

½ bunch of mint, roughly chopped

Chilli flakes

1 pack Vietnamese rice paper sheets, available in most international food stores

1 pack rainbow chard, we use organic

1 pack edible flowers

1 pack rose chai sprouts

Method

Soak the cashew nuts and goji berries in the orange juice for 20-30 minutes. Following this, remove both the nuts and berries from the excess liquid and blend together to form a paste. You will need to add some of the orange juice to help reach this consistency.

Next carefully slice the avocado and sweet mango into small chunks, then deseed and shred the raw Thai papaya using the coarse side of a cheese grater. Tip each of these ingredients into a bowl with the paste. Add the orange blossom water, bean sprouts, tamari and some chopped fresh mint and mix together. Sprinkle in a few chilli flakes to taste. You can add some fresh lime if you like it more zesty.

To assemble

Soak a rice paper sheet in a bowl of boiling water for around 30 seconds. Place on clean surface before lying it on some rainbow chard leaves. Add the mixture on top and roll into shape. Slice the roll into bite size pieces before arranging carefully on a serving dish.

Garnish with edible flowers, rose chai sprouts and more fresh mint and serve with love and devotion. As our chef likes to say: 'If one offers a leaf a flower, with devotion I will accept.' Lord Krishna

Maya
EL BORRACHO AND MARGARITA

Hundreds are familiar with the authentic Mexican restaurant Lucha Libre but only a select few know that there is a staircase that leads down to a different world. Maya is an extraordinary bar based on El Dia De Los Muertos (The Day of the Dead) celebrations in Mexico. It is a late night, hip-hop and mezcalaria bar, serving only the finest mezcals and tequilas. "Where the dead come to dance, is where they shall drink." Welcome to Maya.

Preparation time: 5 minutes | Serves 1

Ingredients

For the El Borracho:

30ml Calle 23 Blanco tequila

30ml Calle 23 Reposado tequila

15ml Del Maguey Vida Mezcal

20ml passion fruit syrup

15ml agave syrup

20ml fresh lime juice

25ml guava juice

The seeds of ½ a passion fruit

For the garnish:

The shell of ½ a passion fruit

10ml Goslings 151 rum

For the Classic Margarita:

50ml Herradura Plata tequila

20ml Cointreau liqueur

20ml fresh lime juice

For the garnish:

A lime wheel

100g dried chillies

100g coarse sea salt

Equipment:

A tall Mexican glass, a tall cocktail glass is a good alternative

Margarita glass or Coupette

Small measuring spoons

Cocktail shaker

Hawthorn strainer

Small tea strainer

Method

For the El Borracho

Put all the ingredients except the passion fruit shell into a cocktail shaker with some ice and shake well.

Fine strain the mixture using the hawthorne and tea strainers.

To serve

Pour the mixture into a tall Mexican or Cocktail glass over ice and place the empty 1/2 passion fruit shell on top of the drink.

Pour 10ml of Goslings 151 rum into the shell and carefully light the rum – make sure to extinguish the flame before consuming!

For the Classic Margarita

Pour all ingredients into a cocktail shaker with some ice and shake well.

Fine strain the mixture using the hawthorne and tea strainers over some ice (do not over dilute).

For the chilli salt

Combine 100g dried chillies with 100g coarse sea salt in a pestle mortar. Mix and grind. Do not overdo, a coarse texture is preferred.

To serve

Wet the rim of a margarita glass or Coupette and press into the chilli salt.

Pour the cocktail mixture into the glass and garnish with a lime wheel.

Enjoy!

The Pan-Asian
APPEAL

Miyagi is a Japanese inspired Pan-Asian concept serving soul food to a soul soundtrack.

Inspired by their travels throughout Asia and Australasia, Miyagi is brought to you by Alex Hannah, Ryan McMahon and the team behind Lucha Libre. They all have huge respect for old school culinary techniques and methods, many of which are adopted by their talented chefs to create new innovative dishes. Major influences in the inception of Miyagi are ramen master David Chang and sushi expert Jiro Ono.

Miyagi is about breaking the mould. "We were tired of the very restrained, almost subservient nature of the Japanese restaurants we had visited and we wanted to create a vibrant restaurant that had soul and personality," says Alex. The extensive menu at Miyagi manages to touch on not only Japanese but Korean, Thai, Malaysian and Chinese. Close your eyes, cast your finger anywhere on the menu and there is no doubt you'll land on something utterly inspired and delicious. Some might say their ideas are quite outlandish, but they all follow the same pathway – food cooked with lots of heart and soul.

There are no shortcuts in what they do at Miyagi, everything is freshly prepared which can be time consuming but is definitely worth the wait, especially when you can taste it in every mouthful of their tummy-warming laksa or one of the crowd favourites; the sticky beef nori taco. Other hugely popular dishes they serve are the contemporary bao buns, sushi platters, ramen bowls and Mrs M's famous chocolate brownie spring rolls with coconut ice cream. Soon to arrive on the scene is the mind-blowing tempura gnocchi bolognese which is sure to be a welcome addition.

Live music and artwork are also a huge focus in terms of concept design and they enlisted local artists, Cyclops Ape to create the 'Ghetto Geishas' that adorn the walls. Miyagi are soon launching their Soul, Beats, Liquor and Eats late night lounge where they will be serving bespoke cocktails and bar snacks with live soul music to accompany you into the early hours of the morning.

Since opening on Bold Street in 2015, they opened a second one shortly after on Allerton Road and have plans for a third one next year – lucky us!

Miyagi PORK RAMEN

There is nothing more comforting than a warm bowl of ramen, the pork belly
and dashi bacon is a great combination with the intense broth.

Preparation time: 45 minutes | Cooking time: 120 minutes | Serves 4

Ingredients

For the pork:

400g pork belly

100g duck fat

For the dashi bacon:

1 rasher streaky smoked bacon

250ml water

5g kombu seaweed

10g dried shiitake mushroom

10ml Usukuchi soy sauce

For the pork ramen broth:

50ml dashi bacon mixture

1 litre roast pork stock

100ml soy sauce

To serve:

400g ramen noodles

Togarashi (Japanese seven-spice)

2 mooli radish, thinly sliced

4 heads spiced pak choi, thinly sliced

4 spring onions, thinly sliced

4 eggs

4 Nori blue seaweed sheets

Method

For the pork

Pierce the pork belly multiple times, then smother in duck fat. Place in an oven at 120˚c degrees for 120 minutes, or until the meat is tender.

For the dashi bacon

Next roast the bacon in the oven for 15 minutes.

Place the remaining dashi bacon ingredients, except the Usukuchi soy sauce, together into a pan and bring to the boil. Reduce the heat to a low simmer and cook for 45-60 minutes. Once cooked remove from the heat, add the Usukuchi soy sauce and then leave to cool.

For the pork ramen broth

Tip 50ml of the cooled dashi bacon mixture into a bowl. Add 1 litre of pork stock and 100ml of soy sauce and mix together at room temperature.

To serve

Take the ramen noodles and cook them in a pan of boiling water for 3 minutes. Once cooked, drain and transfer into serving bowls. Sprinkle with Togarashi.

Mix the sliced mooli radish, pak choi and spring onion in a bowl and place on top of the noodles.

Transfer the pork ramen broth into a pan and bring to the boil. Once cooked, pour into the serving bowls, covering the vegetables and noodles.

Poach the eggs. If you're feeling confident, poach them with the shells on at 62˚c degrees for 55 minutes. Gently crack them open and place on top of the ingredients in the serving bowls.

Remove the pork belly from the oven, portion and pan fry to crisp up, then add to the serving bowls.

To finish, garnish down one side of each bowl with a sheet of Nori blue seaweed.

Miyagi
STICKY BEEF TACO

Inspired by our older brother Lucha Libre we fused our guests favourite Sticky Beef recipe with Mr. M's improvised Nori Seaweed Taco to bring a taco with a bang.

Preparation time: 15 minutes | Cooking time: 15 minutes | Serves 4

Ingredients

For the Nori tacos:

4 Nori blue seaweed sheets

For the tempura batter mix:

250g tempura flour

325ml ice-cold water

95ml rice vinegar

For the beef:

200g of beef fillet tail

200g sweet and sour sauce

50g Sriracha Sauce

For the Miyagi slaw:

¼ savoy cabbage, finely sliced

¼ white cabbage, finely sliced

½ carrot, finely sliced

100g mooli radish, cut into 6cm blocks then sliced thinly

2 spring onions, diced thinly

½ lemon, zested and juiced

½ lime, zested and juiced

To serve:

Wasabi peas, crushed

Kewpie aioli (Japanese mayonnaise)

Micro coriander

Method

For the Nori tacos

In a bowl, whisk together the ingredients for the tempura batter mix until completely combined.

Next take a Nori blue seaweed sheet and cut it into a circle. The best way to do this is to cut around a small bowl.

Submerge the now circular sheet in the tempura batter mix. Remove from the liquid and allow the excess to drip off, leaving a light coating on the Nori sheet.

Put the sheet into a metal taco holder and dip into a pan of boiling oil for 20 seconds. Once the taco is holding its shape, remove from the holder and put drop back into the oil to cook for a further 2-3 minutes or until golden in colour. Carefully remove from the oil and leave the shell to cool and crisp up.

Repeat for the remaining three tacos.

For the beef

Take the 200g of beef fillet tail and cut it into thin slices.

Cover the beef slices in the same tempura batter mix that you used earlier for the taco shell.

Once all the beef is covered, drop carefully into a pan of boiling oil. Fry until crisp and golden.

Whilst the beef is cooking, pour the sweet and sour and Sriracha sauces into a hot pan and reduce down. Once reduced, remove the beef from the oil and mix into the sauce. Reducing the sauce beforehand will help keep the beef crisp.

For the Miyagi slaw

Tip all of the ingredients for the Miyagi slaw into a bowl and mix together.

To serve

Add 20g of the Miyagi slaw mix to the bottom of each taco shell then top with a sprinkle of crushed wasabi peas and a squeeze of Kewpie aioli.

Layer with the crispy beef mix, another drizzle of Kewpie aioli and garnish with micro coriander and a final sprinkle of crushed wasabi peas.

From sausages to
SPIRITS

Expanding from its butchery roots into quality homemade ready meals, deli items, bread, vegetables, wine, beer and spirts, Muffs meets all your foodie needs in Bromborough.

Originally a butcher's shop, Muffs of Bromborough has metamorphosed into a treasure cove of foodie goodies, with traditional butchery – and the family's own sausages and black pudding at its heart.

Today, the shop is a food hall selling everything from meat, cheese, bread and vegetables to wines, local beers and gins, plus an extra special selection of quality ready meals to cook up at home that are made on site. There is also a hot meals and sandwiches counter too.

John Muff's dad Stephen and grandfather Jack began the business in Birkenhead before moving to Bromborough in 1974. In 2016, the shop expanded after moving a couple of doors down the street.

John said: "We're now more of a food hall. It's a much bigger shop.

"The butcher has some very special items now – value-added products like hunter's chicken, chorizo chicken, beef wellington and pork wellington, and marianated chicken and pork. They're hand-made quality produced ready meals that customers can take home and put in the oven."

John started his career training as a butcher at the family shop, before going to run the factory that supplied the local supermarkets with Muffs' sausages. Then he trained as a chef and brought all his experience to the food hall, which boasts Muffs' black pudding and award winning sausages.

"We've won best in the UK for our Old English sausages," he said.

"There are 20 different varieties and they change quite a bit to keep it interesting. At any one time there are around 12 varieties and they rotate on a daily basis."

The traditional butchery remains at the heart of the business. Muffs uses dry ageing fridges to mature and tenderise its beef, which like the majority of its meat, is sourced through a slaughterhouse in North Wales that works with local farms.

The local ethos is also apparent in the other items the shop stocks, from Wirral Gin to in-season asparagus from local growers. And it's proving a long-term recipe for success for Muffs.

"One girl, Gervaise, who works for us now, her grandparents used to come to the shop in Birkenhead, they followed us to Bromborough and they still come in twice a week," said John.

Muffs

MUFFS ULTIMATE BEEF BURGER WITH ONION RINGS, FRIES AND SLAW

We believe in shopping local and helping local people and businesses. Most of the items on this dish come from within our local community.

Preparation time: 30 minutes | Cooking time: 20-30 minutes | Serves 2

Ingredients

2 Muffs ultimate burgers

4 rashers quality smoked streaky bacon

1 large sweet potato

3 large King Edward potatoes

1 beef tomato

Wirral watercress (or equivalent)

1 white onion

125g of flour

Paprika

Panko Japanese breadcrumbs

2 brioche buns

2 bottles Peerless Brewers Hilbre Gold Beer

Smokey chipotle sauce

Your favourite cheese. We use Montagnolo Affine, a fantastic German cheese

For the slaw:

1 white onion

1 small white cabbage

2 large carrots

3 egg yolks

Quality mustard, oil and vinegar

Method

Slice the potatoes thinly and blanch in the deep fat fryer. You are only looking to soften them and put a little bit of colour on them.

For the slaw

While the fries are in, slice the cabbage and one white onion as thinly as possible and grate the carrots. Place in a bowl, season with salt and pepper and mix well.

Make the mayonnaise by adding a small teaspoon of mustard and vinegar to the egg yolks and then very slowly drizzling in the oil while whisking vigorously. If the oil is added too quickly the mayo will split.

After adding about 2 cups of oil you should have a nice smooth emulsion you can now season to taste. Add enough mayo to coat the cabbage, onion and carrot mix.

For the onion rings

Add a teaspoon of paprika to the flour salt and pepper. Start pouring in the beer, whisking well. Mix until there are no lumps and it's the consistency of double cream.

Slice a white onion into rings about 5mm and separate them. In another bowl place your panko breadcrumbs. Dip the rings in the batter then in the panko to coat well. For extra crunch do this twice. Cook in the fryer until they are brown and crispy.

For the burgers

In a thick bottomed frying pan, fry off the bacon until it's crispy then keep warm. Drop the chips back in the fryer to finish them off.

When the bacon is finished, place your burgers in the pan, don't move them around just let them brown off for a couple of minutes. Add a couple of thick slices of beef tomato to the pan and allow them to caramelise.

As soon as the burgers are about half cooked, turn them over and put a generous slab of cheese on top. Turn the tomatoes. Lift the chips out the fryer and pop them on some kitchen roll to soak up excess grease.

Take the burgers out of the pan and rest for a minute on the plate with the bacon.

To serve

Assemble by placing the burger on the bun, then the tomato, crispy bacon and Wirral watercress on top.

Place everything on a plate with a big dollop of slaw. Use the remaining ale to pour a couple of glasses of chilled beer and enjoy!

A view to DINE FOR

Fine dining, afternoon tea and cocktails with 360° views of Liverpool from one of the UK's highest restaurants makes Panoramic 34 a unique experience.

On the 34th floor of Liverpool's West Tower, Panoramic 34 sits 300ft above sea level and boasts possibly the best views of any restaurant in the north, if not the UK, through its floor to ceiling windows.

"Our USP is our location," says Cathy Frost, who looks after front of house at the restaurant her husband opened in 2008.

"We have this panoramic vista right over Liverpool, the sea and out to the Welsh hills. We also have a private dining space which is probably the best space in Liverpool – I'm biased, but it is."

People may come to Panoramic 34 to check out the views but they keep returning for the food. The fine dining menu concentrates on modern European dishes and the afternoon teas served in the cocktail lounge – introduced in response to requests from customers – are hugely popular and booked up weeks in advance. The menus, which include tasting and a la carte, Saturday and Sunday options, are continually evolving to provide new flavours.

Panoramic 34 is a must-visit for foodies taking a culinary tour of Liverpool as well as regular customers.

Cathy said: "Liverpool has become a weekend destination. It's like the United Nations at weekends, sitting in the restaurant or the cocktail lounge you see every nationality and hear every accent, it's not just Scousers – it's everybody."

The way Cathy views the customers is a key part of the welcoming ambience at Panoramic 34.

"I look at it like it's people coming to my house for dinner," she said.

"When I'm meeting people, I have it in my head that it's my friends arriving for a nice dinner with us."

With a career that spanned sales and marketing and estate agency before she studied for a criminology degree as a mature student, Cathy takes a very hands-on approach.

"I love cooking and entertaining at home but it's not that easy," she says.

"At Panoramic I help with the food preparation, I clean the loos. But I don't do waiting on – I'd drop something!"

Panoramic 34
DUCK BREAST, PICKLED OYSTER MUSHROOMS AND CHARRED SPRING ONIONS

A flavoursome Oriental duck dish full of taste and texture that's served in a moreish soy gel sauce.

Preparation time: 4 hours | Cooking time: 45 minutes | Serves 4

Ingredients

For the duck:

4 duck breasts

Salt, pepper and rapeseed oil

For the pickled oyster mushrooms:

1l white wine vinegar

1 tsp salt

1 tsp sugar

2 garlic cloves

Olive oil

½ tsp black peppercorns

1 bay leaf

1kg oyster mushrooms, cleaned and roughly chopped

For the soy gel:

100ml each of soy sauce, sweet soy sauce and cider vinegar

200ml water

5g agar agar

For the charred spring onions:

1 bunch spring onions

Olive oil

Salt and pepper

Method

For the roast duck breasts

Preheat the oven to 220°c.

Gently score the duck skin with a sharp knife. Season the duck breasts with salt and pepper and heat 1 tablespoon of rapeseed oil in a roasting tray or ovenproof pan on top of the stove

Place the breasts, skin-side down, in the tray and fry over a medium heat for 8-10 minutes, allowing the skin to release fat while turning golden brown. Turn and finish cooking in the oven for 7-8 minutes. Remove from the tray and leave to rest in a warm place for 4 minutes.

For the pickled oyster mushrooms

Place all of the ingredients except the mushrooms into a saucepan and add 500ml water. Bring to the boil and add the mushrooms. Cook for 12-15 minutes, or until cooked through.

Remove the mushrooms from the pan with a slotted spoon and set aside to dry on a clean tea towel for 3-4 hours, or until completely dry.

Pour some olive oil into a 1 litre sterilised jar, add the mushrooms, and then cover with more olive oil. Stir together gently until all of the mushrooms are coated in the olive oil. Cover tightly with a sterilised lid.

For the soy gel

Combine the soy sauces, vinegar and water in a small pan and bring to the boil. Remove from the heat, stir in the agar agar and return to the boil to thicken.

For the charred spring onions

Clean the spring onions, leaving them whole with the roots on, trimming the very tops only if they're dry. Sprinkle with a little salt and light olive oil and place on a very hot barbecue or griddle pan for about 2 minutes until charred, then turn and char the other sides equally.

To serve

Plate up the duck breasts and spring onions, add a generous serving of drained oyster mushrooms and dress with the soy gel.

Wines that SING

Tucked away close to the city centre, R&H Fine Wines is an Aladdin's Cave of specialist wines specially sourced by owner Devin Stewart.

Musician-turned-wine merchant Devin Stewart decided to "do something serious" when he became a dad to twin girls – and when couldn't think of something serious, he opened the only independent wine merchant in Liverpool.

He said: "I worked in bars and restaurants over the years and I've always had an interest in wine through my brother (a chef) and my father and uncle – but until five or six years ago, I was pursuing a different career entirely."

R & H Fine Wines – or Roberts & Henry, to give the business its full title – specialises in quality, handmade wines which "lean towards" the organic and biodynamic.

"I'm not an evangelist. Personally, I look for balance and a bit of tension above all and I certainly don't insist on organic and biodynamic – but handmade wines tend to skirt around that road," says Devin, who is originally from Nova Scotia but has lived in Liverpool and Scotland, "and a few places in between".

Biodynamic wines are sort of 'supercharged' organic wine that celebrate their locality, thanks to the farming methods used to grow the grapes.

Devin said: "I've latched on to the idea that great wine is made in the vineyard as opposed to winery – and that as long as it's good and healthy and alive with nature, the wines will sing more of the place that they're from.

"Terroir. It's a French word; it's more than just the earth. The winemaker's goal is to express the traditional flavours of their region, through the fruit of the land and the weather of that year. It celebrates variation."

R & H Fine Wines sells both as a wholesaler and as retailer from its shop in a quirky lane in the business end of the city centre

The majority of the wines on the shelves are 'Old World' European, which Devin selects for quality. He's travelled to Spain, France and Italy on sourcing trips, and enjoys the opportunity that working in wine gives him to meet people.

Devin said: "We've just opened a smaller retail outlet on the other side of town with our partners at the Buyers Club, off Hardman Street – and we're doing more and more wholesale as well, shipping our own and working with some fantastic importers. I'm pretty pleased with the offering just now and there are a couple of irons smouldering away in the fire for 2017."

"There is an energy around the growing food and drink scene in Liverpool and there's a fantastic community of independents to go with it – it's been a real pleasure to be a small part of that over the last few years. The city is on great form."

A wine merchant RECOMMENDS

"When it comes to the classics I'm always happy to see the white Burgundies from Bret Bros, Rioja from Remelluri and the great Super Tuscans," says Devin Stewart, "but these are a few of my favourite things....."

Vitor Claro 'Foxtrot'

A recent addition to the range, it's an elegant field blend from Portalegre in the Alentejo, Portugal. A little Arinto in the mix gives this luscious wine a real lift. I'd say it had a little Burgundian air about it and, like so much of what Portugal has to offer, it's very reasonably priced.

Rubor Viticultores 'Chass!'

Natural wine makers from Cebreros. We ship all of the Rubor wines after a chance meeting a couple of years ago. The Chass! was the first wine I tasted with them and I love it. Made with the Chasselas grape it's a bit left field and a little cloudy but it's full of energy and loaded with flavour.

Clau du Nell Grolleau

The name Leflaive goes before itself as one of the more famous estates in Puligny Montrachet but I've always had a soft spot for this side project near Angers in the Loire Valley, and in particular the Grolleau. The winery has such a beautiful story and the Grolleau is such a quiet, elegant wine that just keeps on giving.

Bodegas Ponce, 'Reto' Albillo

This is a long standing favourite of mine. It pretty much encapsulates what I love about wine. A little known grape, very much of its place (Manchuela), and a wine made very much by hand. It's got weight – but it's fully toned and the fruit is beautifully refined and persistent.

Clos du Gravillas, Rendez Vous Sur La Lune

This is billed by the makers as a red Minervois from the moon. Who needs more than that. It's just so alive and inviting – but still pretty serious and complex. There's no oak used so the fruit really sings. I've been lucky enough to meet John Bowjanowski a few times over the years and he's as charming as his wines.

Nanclares Albarino

I was fortunate enough to visit Nanclares on a trip to Galicia and he absolutely stole my heart. Such a quiet, humble man making some very serious wines. The Crisopa Albarino is one of my all time favourite wine experiences – sharing the wine over lunch with the man who made it. Perfection. I'd go back tomorrow if I could. I don't think Crisopa is available in the UK yet but when it is I'll be there and willing to share.

Johan Meyer, Mother Rock Wines, Mount Abora

I could happily retire to the Swartand region of South Africa and if I had to pick one of the many wine makers blazing trails out of there it would be Johan Mayer. I seem to find my next favourite wine wherever he turns up. Elegance and complexity are the recurring themes throughout his wide ranging portfolio of beautiful wines.

Refreshment across THE MERSEY

The Refreshment Rooms on the banks of the Mersey was due to be demolished in 2011 but the team that stepped in to rescue this Victorian pub have transformed it into a busy, must-visit venue on the Wirral.

Originally opening for business in the 1880s as a meeting place for the passengers using the old Mersey ferry, The Refreshment Rooms today is known as a stop-off point for great food and real ale.

The pub traded until the 1970s, when its name was changed to The Admiral but it gradually fell into disrepair and it ended up empty for five years with the threat of demolition hanging over it.

Plenty of TLC and investment rescued the pub, which reopened in 2012 under its original name, and as manager and now owner Ian Joyce says, it "rose like a phoenix on the banks of Mersey."

Ian, who has run the pub since its reopening and has owned it with a partner since 2015, said: "The Refreshment Rooms has always put a massive emphasis on locally sourced ingredients, working closely with local growers, farmers and suppliers."

"We try to use local microbreweries for cask ales and have a good relationship for the rest of our bar supplies with JW Lees family brewers of Manchester."

Ian and the team, led by Millie, Fil and Liam together with head chef Matty Fairbanks and kitchen team, Steve, Luke, Lexi, Kyle and Ollie, together with kitchen porters led by Mike Galvin have won a top reputation for great home cooked, local produce at value for money prices on the Wirral and beyond.

The pub has a relaxed ambience where kids are welcome. The sunny enclosed beer garden has a kids' play area and there's also a children's section on the menu. Inside, the dining room is light, airy and laid back.

The Refreshment Rooms has a packed weekly agenda with steak nights on Mondays, Tuesday burger nights, over-60s deals from Monday to Wednesday, and live music on Fridays. It's also a popular celebration venue for weddings, christenings and wakes. The Refreshment Rooms serve food 7 days a week 12pm-9pm and also serve breakfast 9am to midday every Saturday and Sunday.

Ian said: "What we've done with The Refreshment Rooms is proving really popular with the punters."

"We've been voted the best pub for food in the whole of Merseyside on TripAdvisor and we've also been awarded 'pub of the season' for our real ale from CAMRA."

So whether the refreshment you require is in food or alcohol form, you're set to be served up a treat when you visit The Refreshment Rooms.

STORNOWAY BLACK PUD AND CHORIZO HASH

A hearty starter or lunchtime snack, made with local black pudding and spiced up with Worcestershire sauce and plenty of black pepper.

Preparation time: 5 minutes | Cooking time: 30 minutes | Serves 4

Ingredients

250g waxy potatoes

120g Stornoway black pudding or a good local black pudding

100g chorizo sausage

1 small onion or large shallot, chopped

10g butter

2 tbsp Worcestershire sauce

Black pepper

4 duck or hen's eggs

Method

Peel the potatoes and cut into 1cm cubes. Cut the chorizo and black pudding to 1cm cubes.

Soften the finely chopped onions or shallot in butter, then add the chorizo and potatoes.

Cook on a medium heat until the potatoes start to break down, then fold the black pudding into the mixture.

Add the Worcestershire sauce and season with the black pepper.

Split the mixture between 4 small ovenproof bowls and bake for 10-15 minutes at 170°c.

Remove the hash from the oven and poach the eggs in boiling water.

To serve

Put a poached egg on top of each bowl of hash. Add a final twist of pepper to each and serve.

Liverpool's Underground DINING CLUB

The Secret Diners Club is a one-of-a-kind dining concept that takes place in unique and unconventional locations around Liverpool.

The concept first came to fruition when Daniel Heffy and Michael Harrison, both highly talented chefs, met whilst working in the kitchen at The London Carriage Works. It wasn't long until the lads started to brew potential ideas and the first Secret Diners Club was in the planning process. After a number of events, PR and event promoter Joe Earnshaw joined to spread the word – the rest is history.

The location of the dinners remain a secret right up until the day of the event when diners receive a text revealing the address and how to get there. Their 6-course fine dining menus are also kept undisclosed right up until the final plate leaves the pass. Throughout the dinner, guests are encouraged to interact and guess the courses on blank menus handed out at the start of service until the actual menu is revealed at the end of the night.

Often they will take inspiration from the surroundings and history of the location and building before curating the menu. From railway stations and lock-ups to warehouses and churches, they have welcomed guests to a wide variety of weird and wonderful locations across the city.

One event took place in Edge Hill train station, which the organisers unveiled by taking guests on the short train journey across to the dinner from Lime Street station. "There were logistical concerns but in the end we took the risk and it was definitely worth it – the atmosphere on the train was phenomenal," says Daniel Heffy.

The dinners are now in huge demand and sell out within minutes – however, this has not always been the case and the founders think the success of their dinners is probably down to this fact – as chefs Michael and Daniel have had around two years before the exposure to experiment, tweak and perfect the concept.

Secret Diners Club is a huge step in the right direction for the Liverpool food scene, the lads hope to branch out further into the North West soon and although it's a 'secret', it's too good to not talk about.

Family-run
FOODIE PUBS

With three pubs that are all within close reach of each other on the Wirral, Stange & Co has refreshment all sewn up.

If you're familiar with the Wirral, it's likely you'll have visited at least one of Stange & Co's pubs: The Ship in Parkgate, The Fox & Hounds in Barnston and The Jug & Bottle in Heswall.

"Due to the Wirral being a peninsula, you are never too far from anywhere," says Zoe McLennan, marketing manager, whose grandad, Bill Rowlands, converted the long established family greengrocers to a pub business over 35 years ago. He built the first one, The Cottage Loaf in Llandudno himself using various locally salvaged materials. Now the company has seven venues across the Wirral, north and mid Wales.

The Ship enjoys a superb location on the front at Parkgate where visitors can enjoy fantastic coastal views over to the mountains of North Wales. It's known for its foodie ambience, real ales and log fire. There are 25 guest rooms at the pub, and a menu that's packed with tasty British classics and seasonal specials, with locally sourced ingredients including meat from Williams of Flint, Wirral watercress and asparagus from Claremont Farm in Bebington.

The 16th century Fox & Hounds in Barnston is a traditional pub, and landlord Ralph has been at the helm for over 30 years since Stange & Co took it on.

It's a real country pub with an oldie-worldly feel that still has a snug bar and a separate lounge. There is a lovely beer garden and the snug bar is dog-friendly. When you go in, it's quite quirky; some things have never changed and stay true to the historic characteristics of the building.

The Fox & Hounds is known for its great food and real ales and has won a number of CAMRA awards for quality.

The Jug & Bottle in the centre of Heswall won the Wirral Taste Award in recent years for its unique menu and use of local produce. It has a reputation as a foodie pub and serves local game in season as well as sourcing other ingredients as close to home as possible. It's also known for serving great real ales.

Like The Ship, guests can stay over at The Jug in one of its six guest rooms, enjoying a central yet secluded location surrounded by peaceful gardens. Some big changes to expand the food offer at The Jug are taking place, which are set to make it even more of a must-visit if you're looking for a top quality pub meal.

The three pubs are within five minutes of each other and they're known locally as dining destinations. The menus are very much individual but with a similar style. The head chefs have creative control but all have the same ethos on the food: seasonal, local produce meaning that the menus change regularly to fit in with the latest tastes of the season.

Stange & Co
BLACK PUDDING AND BRAISED HAM SCOTCH EGG

This is a flavoursome alternative to a classic dish that mixes home-braised ham and black pudding with the traditional sausage meat that's become a firm foodie favourite.

Preparation time: 24 hours plus one hour chilling time | Cooking time: 10 minutes | Serves 1

Ingredients

1 ham hock – you will need 25g of the cooked meat per Scotch egg

25g black pudding, cooked

25g sausage meat

1 free-range egg

Breadcrumbs

Plain flour

Method

Cover the ham hock in water and braise in the oven at 120°c for 24 hours. Once cooled, remove the braising liquid and shred the ham hock, removing any fatty content.

To assemble

Take 25g of shredded ham, 25g of crumbled black pudding and 25g of sausage meat and combine together thoroughly.

Soft boil an egg for 5½ minutes and cool rapidly in iced water. Peel the shell off the egg.

Cut a piece of cling film roughly 6 inches square. Take the ham hock mix and flatten onto the cling film in a circular shape approximately 4mm thick.

Place the egg in the middle of the ham hock mix and lift the edges of the cling film so that the ham mix completely surrounds the egg. Twist the cling film to hold the shape and refrigerate for at least one hour.

To serve

Remove the Scotch egg from the fridge and take off the cling film wrap, add pane by using flour, egg wash and finally breadcrumbs.

Deep fry the breaded Scotch egg for approximately 4 minutes until crisp and golden brown, then slice in half.

Serve with sweet potato fries, dressed leaf salad and homemade brown sauce.

Dining in the CANOPY

Fresh, locally sourced produce throughout a diverse menu suiting each customer who walks through the door.

Tree House originally opened in 2012 as part of the accomplished family who own Fat Italian and So Salsa. In May 2016 they decided to sell and chose the Peters family as the perfect successors. Andy, Tom and Danielle, who are all from Crosby, have previously worked in Fat Italian, So Salsa and Tree House so they know the customers and area like the back of their hands.

Andy runs the restaurant alongside his father Gary, his brother Tom is the chef and life-long friend Danielle is the manager and also heavily involved in the operation of the restaurant. The first thing that strikes you upon entering is the huge overhanging tree decorated with twinkling string lights – it dominates the entire dining area so you get the feeling that you are nestled inside a treehouse. Intimate and cosy is the best way to describe Tree House, the quaint venue can't fit huge amounts of tables in but it allows the staff to give each and every customer their full attention.

"With Crosby being a small area, we know a lot of our customers on a first-name basis and we love getting to know all of them!" says Andy.

The team get together regularly to brainstorm ideas for the specials board which changes weekly, head chef Luke often uses this as an outlet to get creative and trial new recipes – more often than not it's a success. Their sea bass seafood risotto is a fan favourite, probably because they use the freshest of fish from the Fleetwood market, washed down with a cuppa from Crosby Coffee or wine from Mullwood's – diners are truly spoilt for choice. They also recently started serving roast dinners on Sundays which has already proved to be a winner.

Many tourists visit the spectacular sculptures by Antony Gormley on Crosby beach, 100 cast-iron, life size figures spread out along three kilometres of the foreshore, also known as The Another Place figures. Often they will have a quick browse of restaurants nearby on TripAdvisor and Tree House is an obvious choice for many who want to pop in for an appetizing lunch.

Although Tree House is not in the city centre, it's definitely worth the venture out and with plans to expand we may see a few more Tree House roots surfacing across Merseyside in future.

Tree House
SEAFOOD RISOTTO

This dish was dreamt up by our head chef. Originating on our specials board, it quickly became a favourite of our regular customers, and by popular demand was made a permanent addition to the main menu.

Preparation time: 40 minutes | Cooking time: 50 minutes | Serves 4

Ingredients

For the fish stock:

1 white onion, diced

1 carrot, chopped

1 cube butter

500g fish bones

4 bay leaves

1l water

For the risotto:

1 white onion, diced

4 cubes butter

Extra virgin olive oil

3 garlic cloves, chopped

400g Arborio rice

125ml white wine

600ml fish stock

20 mussels

1 handful north Atlantic prawns

1 whole squid

50g Parmesan

1 handful parsley

8 fillets sea bass

To serve:

1 lemon

Method

For the fish stock

Tip the chopped onion and carrot into a pan with a cube of butter and sweat for 3 minutes. Break the fish bones and add to the pan along with the bay leaves and a litre of water. Boil for 30 minutes and then strain.

For the risotto

Add the diced onion to a separate pan with some butter and oil. Sweat for 2 minutes before adding the chopped garlic. Cook for a further 2 minutes.

Tip the Arborio rice into the pan and cook until the rice is translucent.

Stir in the white wine.

Next gradually add the boiling fish stock, then stir continuously for 10 minutes or until the rice is al dente.

Drop in the mussels, prawns, squid, 2 cubes of butter, and a handful of both Parmesan and parsley. Continue to stir over the heat for 2-3 minutes, or until the seafood is cooked through.

For the sea bass

While the risotto is cooking, place the sea bass fillets skin side down in a hot, oiled pan to cook for 2-3 minutes. Flip the fillets and cook for a further 30 seconds on the reverse. The skin should become nice and crispy.

To serve

Portion the risotto into four shallow bowls, then place two fillets of sea bass on top of each. Finish with a drizzle of extra virgin olive oil and a wedge of lemon.

The village
KITCHEN

Set in the heart of Birkdale, Villaggio Cucina is a friendly Italian café, bar and trattoria that's open from breakfast time through to the evening, with authentic food made from fresh local ingredients.

Lorna Kemp achieved her long-time ambition of opening an Italian restaurant in 2012, drawing inspiration from the years she spent holidaying throughout Italy with her husband.

"The places we visited oozed delicious food and wine," says Lorna.

"Typically, Venice bars and some informal restaurants serve 'cicchetti', a brilliant idea of smaller dishes or snacks, such as tuna stuffed olives. In Florence we had the most gorgeous cappelletti pasta, in Valdiobenne we had sublime lamb ragu and the best pizza in Parma – just exquisite."

At Villaggio Cucina, Lorna brings all these influences together in a restaurant that she's infused with Italian values. She's created a venue that's a hub of the village, with a relaxed atmosphere during the day and a real buzz during the busy evenings and weekends.

Open for breakfast, morning coffee, homemade cakes, lunch and dinner, Villaggio Cucina also has a great selection of wine. Everything is served in a bright modern restaurant where you'll find quirky designs hand painted by a local artist on the walls.

Lorna, who cheffed at venues around the North West for more than a decade, works with her chefs to create an authentic taste of Italy using locally sourced ingredients. You'll find modern and classical dishes such as roast rump of lamb with Mediterranean vegetable bulgar wheat, baby aubergines and cumin sauce and chargrilled chicken breast with tomato concasse, saffron orzo pasta and rocket.

Lorna has worked closely with general manager Mike Bowler and restaurant manager Annalisa DeVergori since opening the restaurant. She herself works with the chefs in the kitchen, cooking up delicious recipes inspired by her Italian adventures.

"I wanted a restaurant that typified Italian values and one that I would want to enjoy myself dining and drinking with friends," say Lorna.

"I hope my valued customers who walk each day through my doors feel the same. A dear customer once said to me that; 'you not only have created a restaurant but a community', another customer said 'your restaurant is the hub of the village, I love coming here'."

Villaggio Cucina

KING PRAWN SPAGHETTI WITH SPRING ONION, CHILLI AND LIME

A quick and easy supper dish that's full of flavour and vibrant colours.

Preparation time: 5 minutes | Cooking time: 15 minutes | Serves 4

Ingredients

400g dried spaghetti

24 king prawns – out of shell (cut in ½ length ways)

2 red chillis, sliced

1 bunch spring onions, sliced

2 limes, juiced

25g fresh chives, chopped

30ml white wine

2 tbsp olive oil

Salt and pepper

Method

Place a pan of salted water onto high heat and once boiling vigorously, add the spaghetti, stirring occasionally until it's al dente – approximately 8 minutes.

In a heavy bottomed pan, heat the olive oil, add the king prawns and sauté for about 20 seconds. Add the chillis and white wine and reduce for 2 minutes. Then add the spring onions, lime juice and the cooked spaghetti, tossing it together and mixing well.

Add a pinch of salt, pepper, and serve, garnished with the chopped chives.

Villaggio Cucina
SEA BASS WITH PEA AND PANCETTA RISOTTO

A flavour-filled rich Italian favourite made with homemade stock and served with pan-fried sea bass.

Preparation time: 30 minutes | Cooking time: 40 minutes | Serves 4

Ingredients

4 sea bass fillets

350g risotto rice

300g garden peas (blitz ½ the quantity in a food processor)

200g pancetta lardons, cooked and diced

100g Parmesan cheese, grated

50g salted butter

1 white onion, finely diced

2 garlic cloves, finely diced

2 tbsp olive oil

For the vegetable stock:

1.3kg mixed vegetables such as carrots celeriac, celery, fennel, onions, parsnips and leeks

1 garlic clove, finely diced

1 bunch flat-leaf parsley

2 bay leaves and a few thyme sprigs

Salt and pepper

1.7l water

To garnish:

Roasted comfit of vine tomatoes – tomatoes roasted at 180°c for 10 minutes with oil

Method

For the stock

Prepare and roughly chop the vegetables and put in a pan with the garlic, herbs, seasoning and 1.7l of water. Bring to the boil and simmer for 20 minutes or until the vegetables are tender. Strain the stock into another pan, keeping it on a low simmer.

For the risotto

Heat the olive oil in a large pan over a low heat then add the onions and fry until soft for about 10 minutes.

Add the risotto rice, stir for a minute or two, then add one or two ladles of simmering stock. Stir continuously over the heat, adding stock a ladleful at a time as each addition is absorbed.

After 18-20 minutes, check for the required 'al dente' texture – the rice should be tender, but with a firm bite in the centre and the risotto should be moist.

Now add the diced pancetta, blitzed peas, whole peas, salted butter and Parmesan, stirring continuously until the ingredients have combined.

For the sea bass

Heat a frying pan, add oil, season the sea bass with salt and pepper and place skin side down into the hot frying pan.

Cook for 3 minutes, then add a knob of salted butter. Once the butter has melted and starts to foam, turn the fish over and cook for a further 2 minutes (the skin side should be crispy).

To serve

Divide the risotto between the four plates and place the sea bass on top. Garnish with the roasted tomatoes.

Villaggio Cucina

VANILLA PANA COTTA WITH RASPBERRY COULIS

Prepared a day ahead of when you want to eat them, these delicious Italian puddings are well worth the wait.

Preparation time: 8 hours | Cooking time: 30 minutes | Serves 4

Ingredients

For the panacotta:

600ml whipping cream

70g caster sugar

2 vanilla pods, split lengthways

1½ bronze gelatine leaves

4 dariole moulds

For the raspberry coulis:

200g fresh raspberries, plus extra for garnish

20ml cold water

75g caster sugar

Method

For the pana cotta

Add the sugar and cream into a pan along with the vanilla pods. Bring to the boil slowly and simmer constantly for 5 minutes, stirring occasionally to help keep the vanilla seeds separate and infuse their flavour.

In the meantime, soften the gelatine in a bowl of cold water, ringing out any excess water.

Remove the cream from the heat and slowly add the softened gelatine, stirring constantly until all traces of gelatine have dissolved completely.

Pass the mixture through a fine sieve into a jug, then pour into the moulds.

Refrigerate for at least 8 hours or overnight.

For the raspberry coulis

Place all ingredients into a pan, bring to the boil then simmer for 15 minutes until the mixture thickens. Take off the heat and blitz, then pass through a fine sieve and leave to cool.

Chef's tip

To remove the panacotta from the mould, dip the bottom of mould into warm water for approximately 2 seconds, then turn the panacotta upside down onto serving plate.

Serve the panacotta with the coulis, garnished with fresh raspberries.

Eat to a
SAMBA BEAT

Viva Brazil brings fun, entertaining dining for all the family to central Liverpool with an all you can eat Brazilian roasted meat concept.

As Liverpool's first Brazilian churrascaria restaurant, serving freshly-carved roasted meat to diners at the table, Viva Brazil introduced a whole new concept of eating to the city.

The fun, social style has really taken off, with crowds flocking to the city centre venue to enjoy a massive choice of cooked meats, seafood and vegetarian options, hot and cold salad bars, and wines and cocktails.

"It's really relaxed," says Gary Parr, general manager for the last four years.

"When we first opened in 2012, no one had really seen anything like it before – we were the first in Liverpool. It's a completely unique dining experience; not the sort of place you'd go for a romantic meal for two, because the waiter comes to your table at least 25 times – which is good if you have nothing to talk about!"

Diners can tuck into as much as they want of 15 different cuts of meat, which are brought to the table and carved for them. Viva Brazil uses a card system – one side is green to signal you're ready for more, and the other is red to show you're resting.

Based on Castle Street – one of the 11 original streets in Liverpool – in a listed building, the restaurant has an authentic Brazilian flavour with bright vibrant colours and burnt wood décor.

The South American feel is extended to the drinks, which include caipirinha – Brazil's national cocktail – and guarana, which is native to the Amazon and known for its help in curing hangovers.

Viva Brazil is popular with families and has special deals for children, including an eat for free special for under-10s. There's always something going on to keep the little ones entertained, whether that's magicians, face painters, balloon modellers or samba dancers.

"Kids love it," Gary says.

"We've had them wanting to walk around with the waiter and help serve the customers. It's something different for them to look at – they love the whole theatre of it as well."

Viva Brazil
BRAZILIAN CHEESE BREAD

Pão de Queijo – or Brazilian cheese bread – is a popular breakfast choice or snack in Brazil. These authentic bread balls are easy to make and are yummy served warm from the oven.

Preparation time: 10 minutes, plus 15 minutes chilling | Cooking time: 20 minutes | Makes 25 puff balls

Ingredients

250g tapioca flour or starch (available from Matta's on Bold Street)

150ml milk

75ml oil

1 large or 2 small eggs

330g mature cheddar, grated

Oil for greasing

Salt to taste

Method

Preheat the oven to 200°c.

Place the flour in a large bowl and set aside.

In a medium saucepan, add the milk, oil, salt and bring to the boil. Remove from heat and pour all over the flour in the bowl. Stir it with a spoon (not a whisk) vigorously.

Let cool a little, then add the eggs one at a time waiting until each one is completely incorporated before adding the next.

When the dough is sticky and glossy, stir in the cheese.

Grease your hands and start forming the dough. Use a tablespoon as a measurement for creating individual balls. Make sure to keep your hands very greasy throughout. Then place the balls onto the baking sheet 3cm apart.

Place the baking tray with the balls in a cold dry place or in the fridge for about 15 minutes to make them firm and keep their shape. If you don't want to bake all of them at the same time, place the remaining ones in the freezer to use later.

Bake for 20 minutes until the balls have risen in volume and are golden and crispy on top.

Serve while still warm.

Viva Brazil
BRAZILIAN SALMON STEW

Moqueca de Salmão – or Brazilian salmon stew – brings together vibrant colours and flavours in a hearty fish dish that works well with the Brazilian cheese bread recipe.

Preparation time: 10 minutes | Cooking time: 20 minutes | Serves 4

Ingredients

4 fresh salmon fillets, cut into 2inch pieces

400g mixed peppers, deseeded, destemmed and sliced

35g fresh coriander, chopped

1 tsp salt

Ground pepper to taste

1 fresh chilli pepper, deseeded and chopped

2 fresh tomatoes, sliced

2 medium onions, sliced

2 tbsp fresh lime juice

60ml palm oil

400ml coconut milk

Method

Season the salmon with salt and pepper.

In a medium pan heat 2 tablespoons of palm oil and sear the salmon on the both sides. Take the salmon out of the pan and set aside.

Add the remaining palm oil into the pan, add the onions and fry for 3 minutes. Then add the tomatoes, peppers and chilli and fry for another 5 minutes.

Pour in the coconut milk and lime juice and cook for a further 2 minutes.

Place the salmon back into the pan and cook for 10 minutes on a medium heat, until the fish is thoroughly cooked.

Remove from the heat, add coriander and season with salt.

To serve

Serve immediately, with rice or pão de queijo.

More than a FISHMONGER

The freshest fish, deli goodies and Christmas Kelly Bronze turkeys are the hallmarks of Ward's Fish, a family-run fishmonger and more based at Birkenhead Market.

Now in the hands of the fourth generation of the family, Ward's Fish has been in business for almost a century.

Started in 1927 by Emily Ward, the current incumbents are brothers Nigel and Simon Buckmaster, who run the thriving fishmonger's stall from its base at Birkenhead Market, where it's been since 1976.

Daily fresh fish supplies arrive at the stall, which stocks in the region of 200 types of fish, from live lobsters in a tank to sashimi grade tuna. Selling directly to the public and to around 30 different restaurants, hotels and catering establishments, nothing is on display for more than a couple of hours.

Simon said: "We purchase daily from local wholesalers and directly from British ports including, Peterhead, Fraserborough, Newlyn, Brixham, Whitby, Eyemouth, Tarbert on the banks of Loch Fyne and we import varieties which are not native to our waters three times per week.

"When we buy our stocks, it's from companies and individuals we have been dealing with for years. It comes down to trust and long standing relations.

We are often asked "when does your fish come in?", That is primarily not really the important issue. If something came in this morning, but it was caught a week ago, then the fish is at the end of its life. We can state when the fish was actually caught, giving you a better idea. Supermarket traceability can be a little vague, whereas the fundamental difference between the fish which we stock and fish offered for sale elsewhere is that we have full traceability straight back to the boat which caught it. Our fish is always selected, cut, packed and prepared to the customer's individual specification.

"In most ways it's the complete opposite to a butcher, with fish it's more about the speed of getting the fish from the sea to the plate, rather than the time allowed for the maturity of hanging the meat from the field to the plate."

In addition to the massive choice of fish and shellfish, Wards also stocks condiments, breadcrumbs and tins of caviar and foie gras among a wide range of deli products. A daily specials board lists other deli goodies, seasonal suggestions and even venison. At Christmas, Wards also stocks the famous Kelly Bronze turkeys plus geese and capons.

"Traditionally it was always fishmongers who sold game and game birds alongside Christmas poultry, which is what we have continued to do," says Simon.

"These days it's all about selling the best, which we think we do."

Ward's Fish

Ward's Fish
PAN ROASTED WILD
LIVERPOOL BAY SEA BASS

This delicious recipe showcases the flavour of the fish with a roasted vegetable cauliflower couscous and garden pesto.

Preparation time: 15-20 minutes | Cooking time: 45 minutes | Serves 4

Ingredients

For the fish:

4 x 200g descaled wild sea bass fillets

6 x 1cm square chunks of butter

Pinch of sea salt

Fresh basil leaves.

Samphire, to garnish

For the couscous:

1 large cauliflower

1 garlic clove, chopped

1 lemon, juiced

Salt and pepper

1 red pepper

1 yellow pepper

1 small red onion

1 courgette

1 aubergine

3 tbsp olive oil

For the pesto:

3 tbsp each of mint, basil and coriander, finely chopped

½ lemon, zest and juice

½ bird's eye chilli, deseeded and chopped

Juice of ½ a lemon

3 tbsp olive oil

Method

For the pesto

Pour 3 tablespoons of olive oil into a mixing bowl. Add the mint, basil, coriander, lemon zest, lemon juice, chilli and a pinch of salt and pepper and mix with a tablespoon.

For the couscous

Preheat the oven to 180°c.

Cut the cauliflower into small pieces and place into a food processor. Pulse the mixture until it becomes a fine texture. Place the mixture onto a large baking sheet and cook in a preheated oven at 180°c for 20 minutes, turning occasionally.

Dice the vegetables into 1cm cubes. Pour 3 tablespoons of olive oil into a roasting dish. Place the dish into a preheated oven at 180°c. Once the oil has warmed add the aubergine and courgette and coat with the oil. Cook in the oven for 15 minutes, then add the peppers and onion, stir and place back in the oven for another 10 minutes.

Remove the cauliflower couscous from the oven and allow to cool.

Remove the roasted vegetables from the oven and add the garlic, lemon juice and season with a little salt and pepper. Place back in the oven for another 10 minutes.

Remove the roasted vegetables and gently mix into the cauliflower couscous.

For the fish

Place 2 tablespoons of olive oil into a heavy bottomed pan and put on a medium heat. Gently rub a pinch of sea salt into both sides of the fish.

Once the oil has warmed, place the fish fillets into the pan skin side down. Gently apply a little pressure holding the flesh side of the fish and pushing it downwards. Allow to cook for around 4 minutes until the skin starts to crisp.

Turn the fillets over and place the butter into the pan. Once the butter starts to foam, spoon it over the skin of the fish.

Place the pan into the oven and roast for 2 minutes.

Remove and place the fillets on kitchen paper to rest for a minute.

To serve

Plate up the sea bass fillets on top of the couscous and spoon a little pesto around the sides. Garnish with samphire and fresh basil if desired.

This recipe also works well with wild sea trout, hake or halibut.

The DIRECTORY

These great businesses have supported the making of this book; please support and enjoy them.

Alma de Cuba
St Peter's church
Seel street
Liverpool, L1 4BH
Telephone: 0151 709 1567
Website: www.alma-de-cuba.com
An eclectic mix of Cuban, Hispanic and Latin American influences that are enhanced with Liverpool's great spirit.

The Art School Restaurant
Liverpool 1
Sugnall Street
Liverpool, L7 7EB
Telephone: 0151 230 8600
Website:
www.theartschoolrestaurant.co.uk
Fine dining at the heart of Liverpool, with local suppliers and ingredients always on the menu.

Artisane
263 Woolton Road
Liverpool, L16 8NA
Telephone: 0151 541 1952
Website:
www.facebook.com/artisaneLiverpool
French patisserie offering 'a little piece of France in south Liverpool'

The French Corner
Barclays Trading Estate
Unit 1, Brookfield Drive
Aintree
Liverpool, L9 7AJ
Telephone: 0151 541 1950
Website:
www.facebook.com/The-French-Corner-Ltd-194893417233533/
Authentic French baker supplying wholesale to businesses across the north west.

Aubergine Café
Blenheim Building
The Crescent Walk
West Kirby, CH48 4DA
Telephone: 0151 625 2662
Website:
www.facebook.com/theaubergineco
A hidden gem in West Kirby known to foodies for its support of local ingredients and suppliers, and its great afternoon teas.

Bakchich
54 Bold Street
Liverpool, L1 4ER
Telephone: 0151 707 1255
Website: www.bakchich.co.uk
This Lebanese restaurant with leather banquettes and high bench tables specialises in street food.

The Baltic Fleet Brewhouse
33a Wapping
Liverpool, L1 8DQ
Telephone: 0151 709 3116
Website:
www.balticfleetpubliverpool.com
Known as the home of Scouse, this pub has a rich history and heritage, and also has its own microbrewery on the premises.

The Baltic Social
27 Parliament Street
Liverpool, L8 5RN
Telephone: 0151 707 1137
Website: www.thebalticsocial.com
Craft beers, punk afternoon teas and a menu of well thought out food in a creative venue where there's regular live music.

Bexleys Craft Butchers
561 Prescot Road
Old Swan
Liverpool, L13 5UX
Telephone: 0151 259 4380
Website: www.bexleys.co.uk
National award-winning butchers.

Burnt Truffle
104-106 Telegraph Road
Heswall, CH60 0AQ
Telephone: 0151 342 1111
Website: www.burnttruffle.net
Small bistro serving modern European food.

Buyers Club
24 Hardman St
Liverpool, L1 9AX
Telephone: 0151 709 2400
Website: www.buyers-club.co.uk
A unique restaurant, bar and music venue, which also hosts a number of private events. Serving small plates, fine wines and cocktails.

Chicha
55 Bold Street
Liverpool, L1 4EU
Telephone: 0151 294 4146
Website: www.chicha-liverpool.co.uk
Authentic Peruvian food in the heart of Liverpool, where diners eat surrounded with genuine décor brought back to the UK from Peru.

Constellations
5-39 Greenland Street
Liverpool, L1 0BS
Telephone: 0151 345 6302
Website: www.constellations-liv.com
A venue in the city's cultural corner where you can eat, drink and celebrate, that's known for its superb weekend brunches.

Crosby Coffee Ltd
Unit 14 Bridge Road Industrial Estate
Litherland
Liverpool, L21 2QG
Telephone:
0151 538 5454 / 07592 114055
Website: www.crosbycoffee.co.uk
Specialist artisan coffee supplier to the trade and public, freshly roasting your beans to order every time!

Cuthbert's Bakery Ltd
103 Mt Pleasant
Liverpool, L3 5TB
Telephone: 0151 709 9912
Website:
www.cuthbertsbakehouse.co.uk
Cosy, wood-furnished tea shop with tiled floors, for cakes, light lunches and afternoon tea.

Delifonesca 'Fonseca's' Stanley Street
Stanley Street
Liverpool, L1 6AF
Telephone: 0151 255 0808
Website: www.delifonseca.co.uk
City centre deli, restaurant and bar with regular wine and spirit evenings.

Delifonesca Dockside
Brunswick Dock
Liverpool, L3 4BN
Telephone: 0151 255 0808
Website: www.delifonseca.co.uk
Independent award-winning deli that's a must-visit for foodies, with on-site restaurant famed for its blackboard specials.

District House
18 Water Street
Liverpool, L2 8TD
Telephone: 0151 236 6141
Website: www.districthouse.co.uk
Luxurious venue with red leather booths, mood lighting, DJs and one of the UK's longest bars.

Edge & Son
61 New Chester Road
New Ferry
Wirral, CH62 1AB
Telephone: 0151 645 3044
Website: www.edgebutchers.co.uk
Family-run traditional butchers, specialising in locally-sourced and rare breed meat, which provides butchery masterclasses for members of the public.

Fazenda
Horton House
Exchange Flags
Liverpool, L2 3YL
Telephone: 0151 659 1183
Website: www.fazenda.co.uk/liverpool
Authentic Brazilian slow-roasted meats and salads, served in a buzzing, interactive atmosphere.

FINCA
The Merchant
23 Parr St
Liverpool
L1 4JN
Telephone: 07760 332272
Website: Instagram.com/fincaliverpool
FINCA is a new Cuban street food restaurant currently serving from The Merchant on Parr Street.

Fraiche
11 Rose Mount
Oxton, Wirral
CH43 5SG
Telephone: 0151 652 2914
Website: www.restaurantfraiche.com
Creative modern French dining in a top-shelf Michelin-starred restaurant.

Free State Kitchen
1 Maryland Street (off Hope Street)
Liverpool, L1 9DE
Telephone: 0151 708 5005
Website: www.freestatekitchen.co.uk
Serving a contemporary twist on American classics.

Fritto
Telephone: 07796 766881
Website: www.fritto.org
Email: lucasanvittore@gmail.com
Authentic Italian street food and catering available at markets and pop-up events combined with a social enterprise using food and cooking to effect change in people's lives.

Gorge'us
7 Lancelyn Precinct
Spital Road
Wirral, CH63 9JP
Telephone: 0151 334 4353
Website: www.facebook.com/
Gorgeus-224664544232475
*Vintage-style coffee shop known for its
fantastic cakes, many of which are gluten-
free, plus its superb afternoon teas.*

Hardy's Kitchen Ltd
80 Banks Road
West Kirby
Wirral, CH48 0RE
Telephone: 0151 625 3011 / 07796
486584
Website: www.hardyskitchen.co.uk
*We aim to bring the traditional but with
a twist, using top quality ingredients, big
flavours and always served with loads of
love!*

Kasbah Café Bazaar
72 Bold Street
Liverpool, L1 4HR
Telephone: 0151 707 7744
Website: www.kasbahcafebazaar.co.uk
*North African dishes in a colourful all-day
eatery, with a bazaar selling Moroccan
furnishings.*

L20 Hotel School & Restaurant
Exeter Road
Bootle
L20 7BL
Telephone: 0151 353 4518
Wesbite: www.l20hotelschool.co.uk
*Provides education and training for the
hospitality industry alongside serving
breath-taking food.*

The Liverpool Cheese Company
29a Woolton Street
Liverpool, L25 5NH
Telephone: 0151 428 3942
Website:
www.liverpoolcheesecompany.co.uk
*Specialist cheese company selling around
200 varieties of cheese, cheese celebration
cakes and offering Cheese School classes for
members of the public.*

Liverpool Gin
Sovereign Distillery
Wilson Road
Liverpool, L36 6AD.
Telephone: 0151 480 8800
Website: www.liverpoolgin.com
*Liverpool Gin is a premium organic
product made from scratch using only pure
certified organic botanicals.*

Liverpool Organic Brewery
39 Brasenose Road
Liverpool, L20 8HL
Telephone: 0151 933 9660
Website: www.liverpoolorganicbrewery.
com
*Liverpool Organic Brewery exists for
just one purpose; to create great-tasting,
handcrafted beers using only the finest
ingredients.*

Lucha Libre
96 Wood Street
Liverpool, L1 4DQ
Telephone: 0151 329 0200
Website: www.lucha-libre.co.uk
*An authentic Mexican restaurant
specialising in street food and taking
inspiration from the restaurants and streets
of Guadalajara.*

Lunya
18-20 College Lane
Liverpool One
Liverpool, L1 3DS
Telephone: 0151 706 9770
Website: www.lunya.co.uk
*A unique Catalan and Spanish deli,
restaurant and bar in the heart of
Liverpool, serving the very best of food and
drink from Spain.*

Maggie Mays Café Ltd
90 Bold Street
Liverpool, L1 4HY
Telephone: 0151 709 7600
Website:
www.maggiemaysoriginalscouse.co.uk
*Maggie May's Café is a family run
business that is home to the most famous
Scouse in the city of Liverpool.*

Mattas International Foods
51 Bold St
Liverpool, L1 4EU
Telephone: 0151 709 3031
Website: www.mattas.co.uk
*An award-winning family business with
an extensive range of vegan, vegetarian
and health foods, also a specialist of
international foods.*

Maya
96 Wood Street
Liverpool, L1 4DQ
Telephone: 0151 329 0200
*"Where the dead come to dance is where
they'll drink". Welcome to Maya, a late
night hip-hop and tequila bar.*

Miyagi
77 Bold Street
Liverpool, L1 4EZ
Telephone: 0151 329 0222

Miyagi
137-139 Allerton Road
Liverpool, L18 2DD
Telephone: 0151 724 2255
Website: www.mister-miyagi.co.uk
*Miyagi is a Japanese inspired restaurant
and that bar that serves soul food to a soul
soundtrack.*

Muffs
5-7 Allport Lane
Bromborough
Wirral, CH62 7HH
Telephone: 0151 334 2002
Website: www.muffsonline.co.uk
Originally a butcher, now a food hall with homemade ready meals, deli items, bread, vegetables, wine, beer and spirts among the foodie delight on offer.

Panoramic 34
34th Floor
West Tower
Brook Street
Liverpool, L3 9PJ
Telephone: 0151 236 5534
Website: http://www.panoramic34.com/
Fine dining, afternoon teas and cocktails served in one of the UK's highest restaurants 300ft above sea level with superb views of the city and beyond.

R & H Fine Wines
12 Queen Avenue
Liverpool, L2 4TZ
Telephone: 0151 345 0306
Website: www.randhfinewines.co.uk
Independent wine merchant stocking a delightful choice of Old World wines, with many handmade, biodynamic and organic wines to choose from.

The Refreshment Rooms
2 Bedford Road East
Rock Park
Rock Ferry
Birkenhead
Wirral, CH42 1LS
Telephone: 0151 644 5893
Website: www.refreshmentrooms.info
Family-friendly pub on the banks of the Mersey serving home-cooked meals made from local produce, and cask ales. Weekly programme of special evenings, including steak, burger and music nights.

Secret Diners Club
Address: It's a secret
Telephone: 07760 332272
Website: Instagram.com/sdc_lpool
Secret Diners Club is an unconventional pop-up restaurant which hosts dinners in some of the city's most unique buildings and locations.

Stange & Co Pubs
The Ship
The Parade
Parkgate
Wirral, CH64 6SA
Telephone: 0151 336 3931
Website: www.the-shiphotel.co.uk
Pub with guest rooms, serving British food and seasonal specials made with locally-sourced produce.

The Fox & Hounds
107 Barnston Road
Barnston
Wirral, CH61 1BW
Telephone: 0151 648 7685
Website: www.the-fox-hounds.co.uk
Traditional pub with separate lounge bar and snug, known for its high quality real ales and food made from local ingredients.

The Jug & Bottle
Mount Avenue
Heswall
Wirral, CH60 4RH
Telephone: 0151 342 5535
Website: www.the-jugandbottle.co.uk
Foodie pub with great dishes made from locally sourced ingredients, including seasonal specials such as game.

Tree House
60 Coronation Road
Crosby
Liverpool, L23 5RQ
Telephone: 0151 924 8838
www.treehousecrosby.co.uk
Small and quirky family run restaurant serving fresh tasty food in the heart of Crosby.

Villaggio Cucina
31 Liverpool Road
Birkdale
Merseyside, PR8 4AG
Telephone: 01704 564564
Website: www.villaggiocucina.co.uk
Friendly Italian that's open from breakfast time to evening meals, serving authentic dishes made from locally sourced ingredients. There's an extensive wine list too.

Viva Brazil
36 Castle Street,
Liverpool, L2 0NR
Telephone: 0151 236 8080
Website: www.vivabrazilrestaurants.com
Fun and interactive authentic Brazilian dining experience, featuring roasted meats carved at the table, salads, cocktails and entertainment.

Ward's Fish
Birkenhead Market
CP, 27
Fish & Country Produce Section
Perimeter Stalls
Birkenhead, CH41 2YH
Telephone: 0151 666 1842
Website: www.wardsfish.co.uk
Family-run fishmonger with huge choice of fresh fish and shellfish, game and poultry including Kelly Bronze Christmas turkeys, plus dried goods and deli.

Other titles in the 'Get Stuck In' series

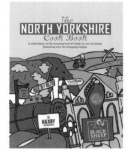

The North Yorkshire Cook Book
features Andrew Pern, Visit
York, Made in Malton, Black
Sheep Brewery and lots more.
978-1-910863-12-1

The Birmingham Cook Book
features Glynn Purnell, The
Smoke Haus, Loaf Bakery,
Simpsons and lots more.
978-1-910863-10-7

The Bristol Cook Book
features Dean Edwards, Lido,
Clifton Sausage, The Ox, and
wines from Corks of Cotham
plus lots more.
978-1-910863-14-5

The Oxfordshire Cook Book
features Mike North of The
Nut Tree Inn, Sudbury House,
Jacobs Inn, The Muddy Duck
and lots more.
978-1-910863-08-4

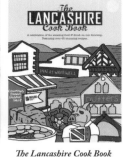

The Lancashire Cook Book
features Andrew Nutter of
Nutters Restaurant, Bertram's,
The Blue Mallard and lots
more.
978-1-910863-09-1

The Sheffield Cook Book
features Baldwin's Omega,
Nonna's, Ashoka, Cubana,
Peppercorn and lots more.
978-0-9928981-0-6

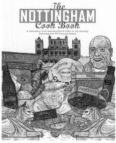

The Nottingham Cook Book
features Sat Bains with
Rooms, World Service, Harts,
Escabeche and lots more.
978-0-9928981-5-1

The Derbyshire Cook Book
features Chatsworth
Estate, Fischer's of Baslow,
Thornbridge Brewery and lots
more.
978-0-9928981-7-5

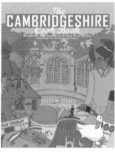

The Cambridgeshire Cook Book
features Daniel Clifford of
Midsummer House, The Pint
Shop, Gog Magog Hills, Clare
College and lots more.
978-0-9928981-9-9

The Suffolk Cook Book
features Jimmy Doherty of
Jimmy's Farm, Gressingham
Duck and lots more.
978-1-910863-02-2

The Manchester Cook Book
features Aiden Byrne, Simon
Rogan, Harvey Nichols and
lots more.
978-1-910863-01-5

The Lincolnshire Cook Book
features Colin McGurran of
Winteringham Fields,
TV chef Rachel Green,
San Pietro and lots more.
978-1-910863-05-3

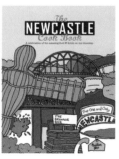

The Newcastle Cook Book
features David Coulson
of Peace & Loaf, Bealim
House, Grainger Market,
Quilliam Brothers and lots
more.
978-1-910863-04-6

The Cheshire Cook Book
features Simon Radley of
The Chester Grosvenor, The
Chef's Table, Great North
Pie Co., Harthill Cookery
School and lots more.
978-1-910863-07-7

**The Leicestershire & Rutland
Cook Book** features Tim Hart
of Hambleton Hall, John's
House, Farndon Fields,
Leicester Market, Walter
Smith and lots more.
978-0-9928981-8-2

*All books in this series are available from Waterstones,
Amazon and independent bookshops.*

FIND OUT MORE ABOUT US AT WWW.MEZEPUBLISHING.CO.UK